I0758821

Autism From Diagnosis to Adulthood: The Spectrum Journey

AUTISM FROM DIAGNOSIS TO ADULTHOOD: THE SPECTRUM JOURNEY

Dawn Ham-Kucharski

With Forewords By

Alex Ham-Kucharski and Rich Ham-Kucharski

ALEX HAM-KUCHARSKI, AUTHOR'S SON AS A CHILD

ALEX HAM-KUCHARSKI, AUTHORS SON AS AN ADULT

Copywrite 2023 © Dawn Ham-Kucharski

All rights reserved.

ISBN: 9798388560988

DEDICATION

This book is dedicated not only to our son Alex, but all the "Alexes" out there who live with autism. To their families, their caregivers, their friends, their partners, their spouses, their loved ones, and to all the professionals and volunteers who believe in all that individuals with autism can be, and for being there, for all of us as we navigate the journey through this spectrum world.

Table of Contents

Prologue

Everyone needs a friend: A best friend, whether you are on the spectrum, a caregiver of someone on the spectrum, everyone. We all need a friend. I've been blessed with the best of friends and family from not only the states I have lived: Michigan, Texas, New Jersey, Georgia, and Oregon, but also around the world—because I had my son. And from the moment Alex was born, or even in utero (that adventure is a whole other story), I've been blessed with a posse of friends who have listened, laughed, cried with me, and asked to learn about, to love Alex and all he can soar to be, but one friend, one best friend, deserves top honors. From the moment we became sisters, inseparable, in August of 1992, she was always taking my hand and pulling me into an adventure that she knew was "just right for you Dawn-er." She always took care of me, and I didn't deserve her. And when Alex was born, she flew in from San Francisco, for a day, after his discharge, sat on my sofa, held all four pounds 11 ounces of him up like Rafiki to baby Simba, and pronounced "he will be just fine."

And one day in 2002, two years after Alex's autism diagnosis (of which the day after I fled to her in San Francisco), Jhoanna Robledo called me from NYC where she and her family now lived. She announced we were co-authoring a book on autism, for Alex; she had an agent for us: Dan Bial, and we were to get to work immediately on the proposal. We had never even discussed this possibility or idea, nor did she ask me if I wanted to. Jho just said we were going to do it. That's that, and we did.

JHO AND ME

After the proposal was drafted, Dan sold our book to Penguin Press, in six weeks' time, and two years later, the now translated also in Bulgarian, Chinese, and Icelandic *The Autism Book: Answers to Your Most Pressing Questions* was published in 2005. What a gift. What time, dedication, passion, and love Jho gave to that writing. The sisters that we were, we had great love for each other—we could also aggravate each other as sibs do—sometimes quite heated (a quote from her in Fall of 2016, as she lectured loudly at me an hour on the phone: "Best friends don't text Dawn-er, they call, they call, phones are for talking"— she was right)—, but our friendship, our best friendship, solidified years before our collaboration, grew even stronger as we traveled, researched, wrote (okay skipped one DC autism conference event to attend a NOW march at the Smithsonian and visit the Holocaust Museum), and collaborated together.

Jho and her husband Will made Alex their family. Raised their children: (Sam, Ben, Nina) to be his cousins, his best friends. Sadly, at levels I still can't fathom the Fates would allow, we lost Jho in July of 2017 to an aggressive, brutal cancer that spread throughout her in a fast rapid storm I had never seen the likes of, just as her daughter was graduating from Princeton. I'm blessed that Will and Ben, Sam, and Nina are still our family, and the world of those with autism, those who work with autism, and their families, are blessed that Jho called me that one day in 2002, and gave "Dawn-er" a command to get researching and writing, that there were other "Alexes" out there that needed us . . . and, no surprise, that Jho, who was a renowned journalist with publications in many periodicals including *New York Magazine*—both in print and video; a creative writer who favored the short story genre; a movie critic; a documentarian; a photographer; a news announcer at WEMU an NPR station; and editor-in-chief for *Brick Underground*, did her last podcast in May of 2017, sharing stories of individuals living in New York City with Disabilities. This book, *Autism from Diagnosis to Adulthood: The Spectrum Journey* would not exist without that first one Jho encouraged us to write.

Resources:

Bonanos, C. (2017, July 20). Remembering our colleague: S. Jhoanna Robledo. *New York Magazine*. Retrieved from http://nymag.com/intelligencer/2017/07/remembering-our-colleague-s-jhoanna-robledo.html

Robledo, S. (2017, September 12). The Brick Underground podcast: Living in NYC with a disability. In *Brick Underground*. Retrieved from https://www.brickunderground.com/live/podcast-navigating-nyc-with-disability

Robledo, J., & Sinclair, A. (n.d.). Sing!. In *Facebook*. Retrieved from
    https://www.facebook.com/pg/Singthedoc/posts/

References

Robledo, S. J., & Ham-Kucharski, D. M. (2005). *The autism book: Answers to your
    most pressing questions*. New York, NY: Penguin.
    https://www.amazon.com/Autism-Book-Answers-Pressing-
    Questions/dp/1583332243

Acknowledgements

So many thanks, hugs, pizzas, chocolates, and beers and wine and bouquets of thanks are owed to our friends and family and professionals who have supported Alex and Rich and I from the United States and Beyond. We are fortunate to know so many incredible people who have been there for all of us individually and collectively throughout our lives and who see Alex as an individual with so many gifts to give this world, who also happens to have autism:

- **The Michigan Crew:** Rich and Alex Ham-Kucharski. Our pets who gave us so much love: Biscuit Billy, Tiffany Marie, and Daisy Mae Ham-Kucharski (the bichon three); Buddy the Chinchilla Ham-Kucharski; Michael and Timon the Hermit Crabs. Dave and Jackie and Emmaline and Caroline Ham and Hobbes and Rusty; Ann and Preston and Evan Kucharski and Dakota Kozik and Electra and Kevin Roszko. Dorothy and Jim Ham. Bill Rose. Verna and Quiller "Jack" Kitto. Newell and Mary Ham. Debra and Marcel Madonna. Sandra and Michael Patelis. Laurie Sample O'Meara. Delores Horton. Lorena Ham. Sheryl and Kelly Henderson. Denise Holaly. Georgean and Jim Kitto. Fran Evans. Sharon Landheer. Joyce and Karen Spear. And all our cousins. Meredith and Ken Kucharski. Grace and Carol Kucharski. Jim and Theresa Grezlak. Lori Duclo Cook. Sarah Shock and Terri Shock. Abi and Chloe and Theresa Desselles. Renee, Nick, and Mitch Sexton. Xinchao and David Li and Hong Zhou. Syed, Aliya, Ali, Aoun, Abid, and Ammar Mehdi. Rhonda and Jennifer Finley and James, Tom, Aaliyah, Alex, Erica, Abby, and Shawn Finley. Maritel and Joshua LeBlond. Monica, Ramon, Ramon, jr., Evelyn, and Vanessa Vingochea. Pennie Socha. Crystal March and Omari Poulson. Mireya Martinez, Briana, and Bianca Soto. Charmaine Johnson-Fuller and Marcus Fuller and Family. Tali and Julian Wendrow. Nikki Rosen-Lieberman and Jacob Lieberman. Lori Hockridge Bohy Hanna and Keith and Kevin. Vanilza DosSantos. Tara Somervell. Jennifer Guglielmi. Leslie Maahs. Kim Kemp-Spears. Soo Son Thompson. Lisa Kiessel-Byrne. Brian Smith. Jessica and Dawn Noyes. Roger Pierce. Sean Frazier. Jim Foster. Brian King. Calixto and Sandie Gonzales. Scott

Truskowski. Josh and Chantel Franks. Mary Kay Herr and Carol Bachmann and Jane Hasse. The Ladies Night Out Group. Dr. Susan Youngs. Dr. Richard and Linda Solomon. Sally Burton-Hoyle. Leonore Gerstein. Diane Carter. The Plymouth Canton Schools. The University of Michigan Health System (Dr. Marci Lesperance, Dr. Liza Green, Dr. Linda Balogh, Mary McGuinness and so many!). Liz Sanger Watson. The Futures HealthCore. Sandi Scott. Donna Rickman. Susan Doyle Gannon. Susan Murtagh. Community Living Services. Tiffany Devon. And the man who got "all the cooks in the kitchen" as he called them, Alex's pediatrician: Dr. Terrance Murphy of the University of Michigan.

- **The New York City Crew:** Jhoanna, Will, Nina, Ben, and Sam Wade. Ellen Goldberg. Jan Carr. Alex Sinclair and Ken Krimstein. (By way of the Upper Midwest). Candace Wade (By way of Tennessee).

- **The Luggage Gang:** Eleanor Anthony, Megan Holt, Suzi Jones-Alaniz, Carolyn Westfall Masini, Marianne Banas.

- **The Texas Crew:** Antares and Jay Leask and Family. Gayle and Don Nunham. Anita and Sean Burrell. The Martin Family. Andy and Tara Heflin. Janell Jarrett. Kelly Miller. Greg Gengo. Laurie Holladay. Heather Borden. Carol Carver Merritt. Plano School District. May Wong.

- **The New Jersey Crew:** Marla Malinauskas. New Providence Middle School. Marla Napurano. The Coyle Family. The Chan Family. Donna Mellusi. Artie Bressler. Elefante Music School. Dr. Steven Moskowitz. Children's Healthcare of Philadelphia.

- **The Georgia Crew:** Sheila and Melissa Beasley and Louie, Mirr, and Disneyanne. Kristin Heaston-Bell. Jon Miner. Misako and Jim Reed. Jason Boskey. Jennifer and Eric Cohen. Kimberly Special Schmidt and Dean Schmidt. Kimberlee, Mackenzie, Madalynn, and Madyson Steinmetz and Elise Rigoletti. Hope and Wesley and Sherry Patterson. The entire Buford Hwy, Cumming GA Waffle House. Jacqueline and Dave Graves. Lydia Kefauver. Mack, Linda, Gavin Butler, and Cassie. Kelleye and Skip Rye. Brad and Elaine Carlton. Michael and Teresa Graham. Allie Roberts and John Fagan. And all our friends at Grove Park. Molly and Jonathan

Switzer. Matthew Lunsford. Amy, Michael, Samantha, and Ben Kessler. Greg, Tammy, and Kyle Galloway. Lynn, Dustin, and Timothy Brecht. Velvie Brady and Ben Harris. Peter, Leigh, and Andrew Eworonsky. Anne Goulart. Nikole F. Smith-Toptas and Mr. "T." Sherry Hassler. Heather Moore. Bretta Milner Smith, Wesley, and Brendan Smith. Lynn, Steve, and Josh Kirby. Edie Ahola. Darrith Russell. Linda and Dayley Fitzpatrick. Paige Franklin Fouts. Janet and Anna Blethen. Patrick Miller. Patty McGinley-Fairley and Colin Fairley. Gay and Dylan Hall. Carey Morris Lewis. Tina and Maranda Hillmer. Doug, Lee Ann, and Carson Mooney. Sarah and David DeJarnette. Cindy, Tommy, and Sarah Costello. Dana, Greg, and Morgan Westbrook. Mark Keesee. Laura Williams. Denny Fitzpatrick. Sue Criswell Gantick. Alison Compton. Lee Ann Broscher. Sharon Lee. Regina Maddox. Jennie Campbell Meredith. Sheree Crowe. Cade Smith. Alex Perez. Umber Hanief. ERACE Atlanta. Forsyth Central High School. John Arundale. Peggy Bryant. Dr. T. Joe Steed. Sid Bramblett. Malone Thornton Vick. Sarah Moore and all of Quota International of Northside Atlanta. Atlanta Rehabilitation and Performance Center, Inc. in Dawsonville. Dr. Ulrike Maria Korte. Dr. Colin Walter. Resurgens Orthopedics. Peachtree Orthopedics. Children's Hospital of Atlanta. Northside Forsyth Hospital. Emory University Hospital. Digestive Care Physicians Dr. Ranvir Singh. Ascend Pediatric Neurology's Dr. Howard Schub. SCAD (Savanah College of Art and Design)-Atlanta. Georgia Gwinnett College. Jennifer Cyers Arrocena. Dr. Mike Stoltzfus. Dr. Ian Curran. University of North Georgia. Dr. Jon Miner. Dr. Sungshin Kim. Tomoe Nishio-Sensei.

- **The Oregon Crew:** Sheila Plummer, Jea French, and Elliott. Alexis Connelly and Augustus. Ginny Buntrock. Virginia Henry. Kevin Jones. Robin Knauerhause. Peter Larson. Paola Landau. Steven Earl King. Crystal Dawn. Pastor Cynthia Dobson McBride. Sarah Stivers. Dr. Gretchen Blyss. Dr. Amber Hincks. Jennifer Locke. Vitalize Acupuncture and Wellness. Jonathan Soffer, Dr. Hans Carlson, Dr. Noelle Teske, and OHSU. Dr. Benjamin Reese and Reese Orthodontics. Dr. Bao V. Pham and Pham Dental Care.

Portland State University. Prof. Chris Cartwright. Prof. Shawn Smallman. Dr. Pronoy Rai. Suwako Watanabe-Sensei. Dr. Priya Kapoor. Dr. Laurence Kominz. The PSU Center for Japanese Studies. Ben Fields. Donna Lauder Chambers and Sebastian. Aimee Apt. Michelle Martine. The entire Castaways Dragon Boat Team. The Gang at Safeway on Jefferson Pharmacy—Our First Portland "Family.".

- **The Global Crew:** Jeannie and Vincent and Irene and Paolo Chang. Maria Fe. Peewee Celino. Yin Yin Chow. Jim and Karen Conlay. Wendy Reuben. Kathie, David, Andrew, and Jacob Duffin. Everyday Miracles Yahoo Group. Children with Autism Yahoo Group. All my students from: Eastern Michigan University; Jackson Community College; Monroe County Community College; Oakland Community College; Central Michigan University; Schoolcraft College; University of North Texas; Texas Woman's University; Collin College; Eastfield College; Richland College; Gwinnett Technical College—for all you taught me.

  Apparently, it "takes a village," a big and wonderful village to keep TeamHK (Rich, Alex, and I!) in line.

  I know I'm missing someone, somewhere—just know we love and appreciate you, too.

Foreward: Life with Autism an Introduction: By Alex Ham-Kucharski

I don't remember much of my childhood due to being a child, but the parts I do remember living with autism are mainly positive memories from kindergarten to

elementary school being around friends with varying forms of autism that I have made a lifelong bond with everyone in my early childhood; and I still keep in touch with some of them today as an adult, I touch more on that point later in the next paragraph. I would play with my friends whether we are at my house, their house, or at the park we all visited in Plymouth, Michigan in the playscape and explore the park from one end of the park to the other end.

Currently as an adult living with autism, I would say not much has changed since childhood, other than moving around the United States from north to south, and from the east coast to the west coast, and I am currently living in Portland, Oregon; and I have currently graduated from Portland State University with a GPA of 3.5 back in December of 2022. I keep in touch with some of my childhood friends who also have autism on my phone via text message on certain holidays and sometimes meet them in person whenever possible when I visit them and family members in Michigan.

From my experiences, I would like to say that it is a different perspective being someone with autism than someone actually seeing and communicating with someone with autism; and it is especially different being someone with autism and have parents that support your decisions than someone with autism but does not have parents that support them at all. I believe that individuals with autism can achieve their dreams with the right resources and support from everyone in their circle of friends and family; this can often lead individuals with autism to grow their talents and intellect in their desired goals; this is what I achieved with the resources and support from friends and family; this also includes my professors and the staff in the colleges I have attended throughout my college career.

Alex Ham-Kucharski, B.A. 2022

Foreward: A Few Words from Dad by Rich Ham-Kucharski

Becoming a first-time parent comes with challenges. You always hear the cliché, "if only good parenting came with a manual". There certainly are challenges for first-time parents to learn the ropes of parenthood. Some seem to be naturals and look like they themselves were born to be parents, others, well you look and think to yourself, "what were they thinking", or "there ought to be licenses for being a parent". But when you throw in some additional challenges like a child with special needs, well that is something even more unique.

Being a dad comes with visions of many typical stereotypes: being the bread winner; teaching your child to play catch (if you have a son, like I do); teaching them all your favorite things to do when you were growing up; dealing with the annoyances of girls; dealing with the wonders of girls; teaching them to drive and maintain their car; how to shave, and so many more.

This preconceived roadmap in your head suddenly changes when your perfect child gets a diagnosis, and when they get the diagnosis of Autism, well that is yet another journey to figure out.

Just when you are convincing yourself that you can do all of these typical dad things, autism changes all of your plans, your strategies, the list of life lessons to be shared. You have to rethink it all. Start from scratch, again. The journey for me as a dad of someone with autism has been challenging, but it has also been one of the most rewarding things I could have ever imagined. For example, early in this journey we were told our son might never even graduate high school with a diploma, and now, he just accepted an offer to Graduate School! He is achieving the "TYPICAL" American Dream, exceeding you in your own personal journey, I only have a Bachelor's Degree.

Dads are supposed to be stoic, brave, and strong, but I have become more empathetic, a better listener, and learned how to think outside the box of fatherhood. That means breaking some of those norms and being more engaged in the emotional side of family relationships, as well as more patient while watching my son learn and grow. It means learning how to say, "I don't know, but I am willing to learn", and how to ask for HELP from others. It also means connecting to other Dad's in the community of autism who are also learning the ropes, sharing lessons learned with newer ones and gleaning nuggets of wisdom from those who are ahead of you in the journey.

Sometimes I feel like Clark Griswold in *Christmas Vacation* when I try so hard to make things perfect only to have the whole world crashing in around you. But other times I also feel like Clark, when it comes together, and all of those 25,000 lights are sparkling bright for the whole world to see.

This is what it feels like to be a dad to someone with autism, and it just keeps getting better with time! Hang in there. Ask for help along the way. And always reflect on the little things that go right, enjoy them, and love those around you with all your heart.

I hope this book will help you and your family on your journey from diagnosis through adulthood, and beyond!

Rich Ham-Kucharski, Dad to an amazing son with autism

Chapter 1 – Diagnosis

Our son, Alex, was diagnosed with moderate to severe autism at 26 months of age on September 5, 2000, and is now 24. Our world is so enhanced by his perspective, and programs like PLAY Project (Play and Language for Autistic Youngsters) involving 30 hours a week of following Alex's lead, helped us to enter his comfort zone, and he to step out if it, and led to speech, lessening of sensory triggers, imaginative play, flexibility from routine, and success for life. Honestly, when our son was around 12 months of age, when that early toddler phase should begin to take hold—curiosity should be blooming—hands should be smashing first birthday cakes with laughter—our son was not. Alex was becoming distant. With that first cake in a crowded room full of family and friends making loud noises and music playing, a cacophony of sensory experiences, Alex pulled himself as far away from that cake in front of him that one can given the limits of a highchair and would not touch it. Rich, his dad, and I chalked it up to a weekend of celebration—"he's tired," we said. He doesn't want to destroy it, we proudly thought.

ALEX'S 1ST BIRTHDAY AND HIS DAD: RICH HAM-KUCHARSKI

Then things began to change. Flashback to BA "Before Alex," and I would see young children in our local Target. Touching things that they shouldn't. Having a meltdown waiting in line, and I thought: if we have children, they will never be like that. These kids were being normal, healthy, neurotypical developing children—but what did this professor know? After that first birthday party for Alex, when he showed no interest in getting into cabinets to bang on pots and pans, or pull everything out, and when he could sit in his "saucer" for hours (as a preemie, at age one, he was just barely 20 pounds, and just sitting up), he would still love to be in that saucer, watching every *Baby Einstein* video in the collection for hours, over and over. I cleaned our home, graded papers, I would smile to myself and think—see, my child, he is so "good."

Know the signs. Alex was born eight weeks premature, at 3 lbs. 4 oz, with sensorineural hearing loss, large vestibular aqueduct syndrome, and mild cerebral palsy from a stroke. In a way, that prematurity and other at birth diagnoses (collectively known as the "Alexisms") helped us to get an early diagnosis of autism when Alex was 26 months old, as so many doctors and educators were monitoring his developments. As research proves, intensive early intervention for those with ASD is vital. And nine years later after Alex's birth, I co-chaired the screening committee on the ASD team at the state level of community health, when Michigan began the steps to mandate insurance coverage for evidence-based practices for individuals with ASD. What I learned as a member of this committee were screening tools, and how to know the signs, which we then implemented across Community Health providers, pediatricians, and educators. The standard signs parents should know, as illustrated from *Autism Speaks* are:

By 6 months

Few or no big smiles or other warm, joyful, and engaging expressions

Limited or no eye contact

By 9 months

Little or no back-and-forth sharing of sounds, smiles, or other facial expressions

By 12 months

Little or no babbling

Little or no back-and-forth gestures such as pointing, showing, reaching, or waving

Little or no response to name

By 16 months

Very few or no words

Autism From Diagnosis to Adulthood: The Spectrum Journey

By 24 months

Very few or no meaningful, two-word phrases (not including imitating or repeating)

At any age

Loss of previously acquired speech, babbling, or social skills

Avoidance of eye contact

Persistent preference for solitude

Difficulty understanding other people's feelings

Delayed language development

Persistent repetition of words or phrases (echolalia)

Resistance to minor changes in routine or surroundings

Restricted interests

Repetitive behaviors (flapping, rocking, spinning, etc.)

> Unusual and intense reactions to sounds, smells, tastes, textures, lights and/or colors. (*Autism Speaks*, 2019)

At a visit to his pediatrician, Dr. Terrance Murphy, when Alex was about 22 months old, and already in speech therapy, his pediatrician reached in and pulled out of his pocket a referral to our local Plymouth-Canton Michigan Schools Early-On Program, and a referral to a developmental pediatrician, Dr. Richard Solomon, and said: "I think there is something going on with Alex besides his hearing loss." My pulse began to rise with the unknown, and I thought "No way, our son just has hearing loss and some preemie delays . . ." Then the dread. The unknown. Dr. Murphy didn't use the actual word *autism* that morning, but a quick yahoo search of Dr. Richard Solomon led to his writings on autism, everything autism, his PLAY Project (PLAY and Language for Autistic Youngsters), and my response was: denial. Waste of time. Our son doesn't speak because he has hearing loss. He is delayed because he had a stroke. He's obsessed with staring at ceiling fans, because well . . . uh . . . I had no answer for that . . . but fear of the unknown, the "what ifs": what would become of our son, his life, the dreams we had had for him, the unknown—it kept me up almost every night as we waited those few months to meet this "Dr. Solomon," who would no doubt take a look at our Alex, and ask us to leave, that he worked only with children with autism, which our son clearly did not have . . . But we would soon learn how so right Dr. Murphy was . . . and the feeling of isolation began to creep in . . .

When Alex was diagnosed in 2000, he was under the *DSM-IV* (*Diagnostic and Statistical Manual of Mental Diseases)*, which categorized a diagnosis of autism as the following:

A total of six (or more) items from (1), (2), and (3), with at least two from (1), and one each from (2) and (3):

Qualitative impairment in social interaction, as manifested by at least two of the following:

a marked impairment in the use of multiple nonverbal behaviors such as eye-to-eye gaze, facial expression, body postures, and gestures to regulate social interaction.

b. failure to develop peer relationships appropriate to developmental level.

c. a lack of spontaneous seeking to share enjoyment, interests or achievements with other people (e.g., by a lack of showing, bringing or pointing out objects of interest.

d. lack of social or emotional reciprocity.

2. Qualitative impairments in communication as manifested by at least one of the following:

a. delay in, or total lack of, the development of spoken language (not accompanied by an attempt to compensate through alternative modes of communication such as gesture or mime).

b. in individuals with adequate speech, marked impairment in the ability to initiate or sustain a conversation with others.

c. stereotyped and repetitive use of language or idiosyncratic language.

d. lack of varied, spontaneous, make-believe play or social imitative play appropriate to developmental level.

3. Restricted, repetitive, and stereotyped patterns of behavior, interests and activities, as manifested by at least one of the following:

a. encompassing preoccupation with one or more stereotyped and restricted patterns of interest that is abnormal either in intensity or focus.

b. apparently inflexible adherence to specific nonfunctional routines or rituals.

c. stereotyped and repetitive motor mannerisms (e.g., hand or finger flapping or twisting, or complex whole-body movements).

d. persistent preoccupation with parts of objects.

B. Delays or abnormal functioning in at least one of the following areas, with onset prior to age 3 years: (1) social interaction, (2) language as used in social communication, or (3) symbolic or imaginative play.

C. The disturbance is not better accounted for by Rett's Disorder or Childhood Disintegrative Disorder. (APA, 2000 as cited in *Interactive Autism Network*, 2019).

If your child was diagnosed with autism spectrum disorder up till 2013, it is likely they were diagnosed via screening tools in coherence with the mandates of ASD in the *DSM-IV*. They were also further sub-grouped into: Autism, Asperger Syndrome (no longer a diagnosis, replaced with ASD diagnosis), Child Disintegrative Disorder (late onset of developmental delays), and PDD-NOS (Pervasive Developmental Delay Not Otherwise Specified), and after further genetic testing possibly Rett's Syndrome or Fragile X. Asperger differentiates as receiving this diagnoses as these individuals, under *DSM-IV,* were categorized as speaking early and having higher intelligence, with social awkwardness and sensory integration issues, while PDD-NOS often referenced those likely to be on the Autism Spectrum, yet without all of the identifying ASD characteristics, and Rett's and Fragile X are genetic conditions (see resources below).

With the advent of the *DSM-5* in 2013, all of these categories referenced above fall under a straight diagnosis of autism, minus Rett's and Fragile X due to their genetic components and are now listed as separate diagnoses. *DSM-5*, as of 2013 using the following criteria to diagnose autism:

A. Persistent deficits in social communication and social interaction across multiple contexts, as manifested by the following, currently or by history (examples are illustrative, not exhaustive, see text):

1. Deficits in social-emotional reciprocity, ranging, for example, from abnormal social approach and failure of normal back-and-forth conversation; to reduced sharing of interests, emotions, or affect; to failure to initiate or respond to social interactions.

2. Deficits in nonverbal communicative behaviors used for social interaction, ranging, for example, from poorly integrated verbal and nonverbal communication; to abnormalities in eye contact and body language or deficits in understanding and use of gestures; to a total lack of facial expressions and nonverbal communication.

3. Deficits in developing, maintaining, and understanding relationships, ranging, for example, from difficulties adjusting behavior to suit various social contexts; to difficulties in sharing imaginative play or in making friends; to absence of interest in peers.

A. Specify current severity: Severity is based on social communication impairments and restricted repetitive patterns of behavior…

B. Restricted, repetitive patterns of behavior, interests, or activities, as manifested by at least two of the following, currently or by history . . .

1.   Stereotyped or repetitive motor movements, use of objects, or speech (e.g., simple motor stereotypies, lining up toys or flipping objects, echolalia, idiosyncratic phrases).

2.   Insistence on sameness, inflexible adherence to routines, or ritualized patterns or verbal nonverbal behavior (e.g., extreme distress at small changes, difficulties with transitions, rigid thinking patterns, greeting rituals, need to take same route or eat food every day).

3.   Highly restricted, fixated interests that are abnormal in intensity or focus (e.g., strong attachment to or preoccupation with unusual objects, excessively circumscribed or perseverative interest).

4.   Hyper- or hypo reactivity to sensory input or unusual interests in sensory aspects of the environment (e.g., apparent indifference to pain/temperature, adverse response to specific sounds or textures, excessive smelling or touching of objects, visual fascination with lights or movement).

5.   Specify current severity: Severity is based on social communication impairments and restricted, repetitive patterns of behavior. …

C. Symptoms must be present in the early developmental period (but may not become fully manifest until social demands exceed limited capacities or may be masked by learned strategies in later life).

D. Symptoms cause clinically significant impairment in social, occupational, or other important areas of current functioning.

E. These disturbances are not better explained by intellectual disability (intellectual developmental disorder) or global developmental delay. Intellectual disability and autism spectrum disorder frequently co-occur; to make comorbid diagnoses of autism spectrum disorder and intellectual disability, social communication should be below that expected for general developmental level.

Note: Individuals with a well-established DSM-IV diagnosis of autistic disorder, Asperger's disorder, or pervasive developmental disorder not otherwise specified should be given the diagnosis of autism spectrum disorder. Individuals who have marked deficits in social communication, but whose symptoms do not otherwise meet criteria for autism spectrum disorder, should be evaluated for social (pragmatic) communication disorder. (DSM-5 Criteria, 2019)

ALEX, AGE 2, AND I, IN HIS EARLY ON CLASS AFTER HIS ASD DIAGNOSIS

Resources (Even region-based resources can lead you on the right path in your own communities)

- **American Psychiatric Association (APA):** *Diagnostic and Statistical manual of Mental Disorders-5 (DSM-5)* https://www.psychiatry.org/psychiatrists/practice/dsm
- **Arbor Autism Centers** https://arborautismcenters.com/
- **Know the Signs:** https://www.youtube.com/watch?v=0idZghw97dc
- **Michigan Autism Council** https://www.michigan.gov/autism/0,4848,7-294-63678---,00.html
- **Early Intervention and IDEA (Individuals with Disabilities Education Act) Laws** https://www.wrightslaw.com/info/ei.index.htm
- **Early On Program Michigan** https://1800earlyon.org/
- **National Fragile X Foundation** https://fragilex.org/
- **Plymouth-Canton Michigan Community Schools IPSEP (Infant and Preschool Program)** https://www.pccsk12.com/about-p-ccs/departments/teaching-learning/specialized-support-services
- **PLAY Project (Play and Language for Autistic Youngsters)** https://www.playproject.org/
- **Rett Syndrome** https://www.rettsyndrome.org/about-rett-syndrome/what-is-Rettsyndrome
- **Screening Tools for Autism** https://www.cdc.gov/ncbddd/autism/hcp-screening.html#Tools
- **M-CHAT-R Autism Tool for Parents, Caregivers, and Pediatricians** https://www.autismspeaks.org/screen-your-child

References

DSM-5 Criteria (2019). *In Autism speaks*. Retrieved July 1, 2019, from https://www.autismspeaks.org/dsm-5-criteria .

(2019). In *Interactive Autism Network*. Retrieved July 1, 2019, from
https://iancommunity.org/cs/autism/dsm_iv_criteria .

Hill, W. (2022). Pushing Play. Medicine at Michigan, 29-34.
https://www.medicineatmichigan.org/sites/default/files/archives/fall2002.pdf

Learn the signs (2019). *In Autism speaks*. Retrieved from
https://www.autismspeaks.org/learn-signs .

Chapter 2 - Early Intervention

Early intervention is the key to living a life that soars for an individual with autism. In their research, Bushhan Gupta, V., Hyman, S. L., Plauche Johnson, C., Bryant, J., Byers, B., Kallen, R., Yeargin-Allsop, M. (2007), tell us that "Early Intervention of and intervention for developmental problems improves developmental outcomes and allays parental anxiety" (2007) when we identify children with autism early, at well child exams and in our school districts using tools such as the M-CHAT (*Modified Checklist for Autism in Toddlers*), which is the standard recommendation of screening for ASD in children age 24-36 months as evidenced in Toh, Wee-Yen Tan, Sie-Teck Lau, Kiyu (2018) as the M-CHAT is "accurate not only in detecting ASD, but also useful in detecting other DD [Developmental Disorders]" (p. 33). I have friends whose children are artists, athletes, graduate students, social, employed, thriving. Our road to early intervention, in a pre-covid world (I recognize that life in covid changes the game strategy—and I will reference that throughout our "conversation" together in this book), began even before Alex's ASD diagnosis when at age 18 months, our pediatrician, Dr. Murphy, handed us a flyer to contact Plymouth-Canton School District's IPSEP Early On program for evaluation. At 19 months, Alex began public school, and a windfall of therapies: OT, Speech, PT, Hippotherapy, PLAY Project, Recreational, University of Michigan Dance Marathon, Challenge Air, Program to Educate All Cyclists (PEAC), Martial Arts therapy, Music Therapy, Yoga Therapy, Chiropractor, Massage Therapy all in our own Michigan backyard of Plymouth, Canton, Ann Arbor, Chelsea, Lincoln Park, Rochester Hills, Westland, Wayne, Garden City, and Dearborn (Futures HealthCore shout out!). We are forever grateful to those early intervention educators, therapists, doctors, staff, volunteers, who led Alex onto all the paths he now walks (and rides!) ...

Once Alex was diagnosed at 26 months of age with autism, on September 7, 2002, the protocol of all hours of our being became centered around the philosophy of "early intensive intervention." The vast and phenomenal screening tools and protocols now available to pediatricians and mandated by many states at certain well child check visits makes early diagnosis very possible and vital and helps to get those diagnosed with autism as early as possible onto similar paths of intervention. Landa, R. J. (2018) tells us in "Efficacy of Early Interventions for Infants and Young

Children with, and at Risk for, autism spectrum disorders" that early diagnosis of ASD is important as:

Once a diagnosis has been made, children with ASD often will qualify for EI [Early Intervention] services. Intervention is needed because they are not developing in social, play, and in most cases, language, and cognitive domains at the expected pace or in the expected multi-modal, integrated way. (p. 26)

And while I am a true believer of such practice, as research shows that we have that small frame window to truly work with children on the spectrum to make leaps and bounds by age six (and)—as it took our child from a non-verbal, social understandings recluse to an accelerated track of expressive and receptive speech, understanding sensory processing disorders, and making developmental milestone leaps, I truly support early intervention, but I am also a believer that any individual with autism—child or adult, can and should continue with therapeutic intervention to enhance their lives and abilities—and such approaches will. That being said, we know that Covid-19 limited access to social community situations for all populations, but for those children diagnosed with ASD and in these early (and most vital!) developmental ages of birth to six, being unable to receive intervention services in inclusive spaces in the community is a unavoidable, and unnerving to say the least for their loved ones, situation. Diamond and Merrick (2022) in their published research "Editorial: Children's Neurodevelopment in the Post-COVID era: From Hospital to Community" address the influence of the pandemic on early intervention services:

ALEX CO-PILOTS A CESSNA OVER ANN ARBOR MICHIGAN WITH CHALLENGE AIR

Any discussion of COVID-19 and disabilities in children would be remiss in not mentioning the special importance of the effect of social isolation on a subgroup of children, already at a disadvantage regarding their communication and social skills, namely children with autism spectrum disorder (ASD)... Indeed, given that anxiety, depression, irritability, boredom, inattention and fear of COVID-19 are predominant new-onset psychological problems in children during the COVID-19 pandemic, children with pre-existing behavioral problems like autism and attention deficit hyperactivity disorder have a high probability of worsening of their behavioral symptoms. (Diamond and Merrick, 2022)

Covid had the entire world scrambling quickly to resee how we interact: whether through our jobs, or schooling, or medical care, or with loved ones. A system of meeting in person for evaluation of possible ASD, creating an educational or intervention plan, involved quick rethinking of all processes. Our world became electronic—Zoom, Microsoft Teams, Google Meet, Instant Messenger Video "get togethers" and the like. And here you are, a parent of a child recently diagnosed with autism, and the option of getting together with professionals or in an inclusive and social environment, is an option you and your family do not have and will forever in some cases be forever changed (even as simple as a McDs' meetup for fries and playscape—gone). IFSP (Individualized Family Service Plans) meetings switched to Zoom, and some still are. In the state of Oregon for example, some areas still provide an option of Zoom or in person round table for planning meetings with educators and families. Therapists, clinicians, and educators were soon working with family via video conferencing. None of this is easy to design and facilitate. Not everyone has the same tools, technology or technology understandings, many do not have access to an internet provider, and public Wi-Fi places like cafes, libraries, fast food establishments were closed during the height of the pandemic. If you as a caregiver were scared, you were not (and are not) alone. Globally, access to intervention services during the pandemic was a fractured shift in how services were provided, from an early intervention standpoint, and older children stand point, for those with ASD. Recent

ALEX HAM-KUCHARSKI IN PROMOTIONAL POSE FOR PORTLAND STATE UNIVERSITY KABUKI PERFORMANCE (PSU CENTER FOR JAPANESE STUDIES, 2022)

research out of India from Mayur Kaku et al (2021) surmised what we parents know: Individuals, especially children with ASD, had heightened anxieties and thus behavioral outbursts during the pandemic shutdowns, all around the world:

> …coronavirus disease 2019 (COVID-19) pandemic is thought to have greatly impacted families of individuals with autism spectrum disorder (ASD) due to lockdown, given lack of access to healthcare, therapy, and day-care centers. This survey was conducted to understand the magnitude of the impact of lockdown, and its effect on the health and behavior of individuals with ASD and their families… Of the 153 families surveyed, nearly half of the individuals with ASD had an inadequate understanding of lockdown, 54% had increased screen-time, while a third reported new-onset behavioral changes. (Mayur Kaku et al, 2021).

Fortunately, as mentioned above, our teachers and therapists and clinicians, our ASD teams of "essential workers" came through. Technologies and texts led to more parents and caregivers being trained in intervention and all worked together as a team. Definitely stumbling blocks and hurdles along the way, tears, anxieties for us all, but we did it. We are here in 2023 and beyond, and we hold each other's hands:

> Early childhood programs and systems were able to leverage existing strengths and recognize opportunities to support more families comprehensively. However, respondents [of a cited assessment] a need for innovative strategies, resources, and collaborative partnerships to realize these opportunities. (Impact of the COVID-19 Pandemic on Early Identification of Developmental Delays and Disabilities and Opportunities for Improvement, 2021)

And while Covid-19 truly is a world my family and I did not live in during our early intervention strategies, plans, and actions with our son, I am hopeful that seeing which interventions were successful for us, can lead to research in your global communities to find similar, even post-covid. In limited space, I am just going to list some of the options out there for individuals living with autism, and I would love for others to reach out to me and share more (correspondence can be sent to: dawnhkspectrumjourney@gmail.com.

For us, Dr. Rick Solomon's PLAY Project (Play and Language for Autistic Youngsters)—that 30 hours a week of following your child's lead (we were in the program with Alex from age 26 months to age six)—entering their comfort zone to help move them into our world was the key—based on Dr. Stanley Greenspan's DIR Model (Developmental and Individuals Relationship Based Model "Floortime), and was a perfect fit for our son and family. Alex also began speech therapy—prior to the diagnosis of ASD—in both clinical, school, and home setting by age 18 months, began occupational sensory integration therapy at age 26 months—also in clinical, school, and home settings. Alex continues, at age 24, to have physical therapy. And Alex has participated in yoga, martial arts, and massage therapy. Alex has been in social groups—recreational and therapeutic (The Futures HealthCore [my old stomping grounds where I was an outreach coordinator and Early On Consultant]). And attended special needs camps at all ages—including a film one just for those with autism in Plano, Texas. We have followed the protocol of the Toronto based *OWL / It Takes Two to Talk* (Observe, Wait, Listen) and *More than Words* programs—per parent trainings at Alex's Plymouth-Canton School District Early On and Pre-Primary Impaired trainings for parents and caregivers; along with sports therapy via Jack's Place for Autism (Michigan), Special Olympics (three states), and Miracle League (in three states). We have participated in university-based Dance Marathon recreational and social therapeutic programs at the University of Michigan and University of North Texas for 11 years. Participated for in as many years with PEAC (Program to Educate all Cyclists) in Michigan—designed to teach alternative transportation for those with special needs. Alex began participating in hippotherapy (age four) at Great Strides in Chelsea, Michigan—horseback riding with an occupational therapist—that has continued his whole life with horseback riding, competing in equestrian at the intermediate level 1 and 2 with Special Olympics Forsyth County and Bearfoot Ranch.

There are also many other scientific evidence based therapeutic approaches for children with autism including the most renowned ABA (Applied Behavioral Analysis) which while not working with a licensed BCBA (Board Certified Behavior Analysts) therapists, was employed as we advanced through PLAY Project and similar technique used by Alex's speech therapists and teachers . . . There is also RDI (Relationship Developmental Intervention), and so vastly many forms of beneficial programs. Before Covid, almost all these services included parent based training as well as intervention work with individuals with ASD—in person—but in the age of Covid, many are also now including a virtual component. Check with your local intervention specialists in your area.

~ 15 ~

And trust me, I have experienced, and our family knows firsthand the deep financial stress the cost of early intervention therapies, and all lifetime therapies cost, for those on the autism spectrum. I remember days in Michigan of asking friends and family for their 10 cents returnable metal cans and bottles, so I could get money for Alex's meds. Gas for our car to go to Alex's appointments. We foreclosed on a home in 2007. I have made many Dollar Tree meals. We celebrated with Dollar Tree steaks on camping grill for July 4ths. And I make a mean Dollar Tree Dinty Moore stew. I've done all my child's gifts from Dollar Tree with returnable cans and bottle money at Christmas' past when Alex was a little guy. There are resources. I served on committee in the capitol in Michigan to mandate insurance cover evidence-based intervention therapies for autism—but that is a state to state country to country determinant. For hippotherapy, Alex's OT provider gave me a diagnosis script to read over the phone to get our health insurance to cover it, and our local Elks Club provided two years of co-pay cost for the service. Easter Seals also offers a variety of evidence-based interventions for kids with autism. Ask. Ask. Ask. Reach out to local community-based service clubs. I know it is daunting. But I believe in you. And I know you can do it!

Finally, service animals and emotional support animals are very beneficial for individuals with autism. At age 21, in 2019, our son Alex's sensory triggers heightened again to lengths we had not seen in many years, and he has even discussed with us, down the road, he would like a therapy dog trained to work with him. These are working dogs that are trained to know an individual's sensory triggers and help steer their human from them while providing calm intervention. As I stated when I began this thread—I would love to hear what other sources of therapeutic intervention those with autism are succeeding with (dawnhkspectrumjourney@gmail.com)!

ALEX AND BISCUIT. WHILE NOT A TRAINED SERVICE DOG, BISCUIT AND ALEX WERE BEST FRIENDS.

Resources

- **M-CHAT-R Autism Tool for Parents, Caregivers, and Pediatricians** https://www.autismspeaks.org/screen-your-child
- **The Play Project** https://www.playproject.org/
- *Autism: The Potential Within: The PLAY Project Approach to Helping Young Children with Autism* http://www.lulu.com/shop/richard-solomon-md/autism-the-potential-within-the-play-project-approach-to-helping-young-children-with-autism/paperback/product-22620946.html
- **Floortime** http://www.icdl.com/dir
- **ABA** https://www.autismspeaks.org/applied-behavior-analysis-aba-0
- **RDI** https://www.autismspeaks.org/relationship-development-intervention-rdi-0
- **Hippotherapy** https://americanhippotherapyassociation.org/
- **Easter Seals** https://www.easterseals.com/
- **Therapeutic Riding** https://myasdf.org/media-center/articles/how-your-autistic-child-can-benefit-from-equine-therapy/
- **Dance Marathon at the University of Michigan** https://dmum.org/

- **Challenge Air** https://www.challengeair.com/
- **Program to Educate All Cyclists** https://www.bikeprogram.org/
- **Music Therapy** http://www.musictherapy.org/assets/1/7/MT_Autism_2012.pdf
- **Yoga Therapy** https://www.ncbi.nlm.nih.gov/pmc/articles/PMC3151379/
- **It Takes Two to Talk: Hanen Program** http://www.hanen.org/Programs/For-Parents/It-Takes-Two-to-Talk.aspx
- **More Than Words: Hanen Program** http://www.hanen.org/Programs/For-Parents/More-Than-Words.aspx
- **Special Olympics** https://www.specialolympics.org/
- **Miracle League** https://www.miracleleague.com/
- **Plano, Texas Adaptive Recreation** https://www.plano.gov/882/Adapted-Recreation
- **Futures HealthCore** https://discoverfutures.com/
- **Magnolia Autism Services, Lacombe, LA Eleanor Anthony: 985-218-9218 A center for ABA, social groups, behavioral therapies, IEP advocacy, and care giver coaching.**

References

Act Early Response to Covid-19 Assessment. (2021). Impact of the COVID-19 Pandemic on Early Identification of Developmental Delays and Disabilities and Opportunities for Improvement . *CDC*. https://www.cdc.gov/ncbddd/actearly/pdf/impact-covid-developdisabil-508.pdf

Bushhan Gupta, V., Hyman, S. L., Plauche Johnson, C., Bryant, J., Byers, B., Kallen, R., ... Yeargin-Allsop, M. (2007, April 1). Identifying children with autism early. *Pediatrics*, 19(1). doi: https://pediatrics.aappublications.org/content/119/1/152.short

Diamond, G., & Merrick, J. (2022, October 12). Editorial: Children's neurodevelopment in the post-COVID era: From hospital to community.

Frontier in Pediatrics, 10.
https://doi.org/https://doi.org/10.3389/fped.2022.976884

Landa, R. J. (2018). Efficacy of early interventions for infants and young children with, and at risk for, autism spectrum disorders. *International Review of Psychiatry*, 30(1), 25–39.
https://doi.org/10.1080/09540261.2018.1432574

Mayu Kaku, S., Chandran, S., Roopa, N., Choudhary, A., Ramesh, J., Somashkeriah, S., Kuduvalli, S., Rao, V. S., Mysore, A. (2021, November). Coping with autism during lockdown period of the COVID-19 pandemic: A cross-sectional survey. *Indian Journal of Psychology*, 63(6), 568-574.
https://doi.org/10.4103/indianjpsychiatry.indianjpsychiatry_344_21

Portland State University Center for Japanese Studies. (2022). Kabuki in English 2022: The Sardine Seller's Net of Love - Preceded by a Medley of Buyô Dances. *PDX Scholar*. https://pdxscholar.library.pdx.edu/cjs/1/

Toh, T., Wee-Yen Tan, V., Sie-Teck Lau, P., & Kiyu, A. (2018). Accuracy of Modified Checklist for Autism in Toddlers (M-CHAT) in Detecting Autism and Other Developmental Disorders in Community Clinics. *Journal of Autism and Developmental Disorders*, 48, 28-35.

Chapter 3 - Comfort Zones

Individuals on the spectrum "perseverate" in their "comfort zones" often with "repetitive behaviors" or "stimming." An individual may toe walk, rock back and forth, script play (my son is often a Power Ranger or *Yakuza*), or have a "place" literal and figurative that is their comfort area—some with autism crave sensory input of deep pressure—heavy blankets, a weighted vest, a bean bag, a rocking chair, a swing, a ball pit, or a hoodie—my son, or for any individual with autism that comfort zone may be an object: trains, movies, music, Legos, cars, monster trucks, dinosaurs, electronics (last two—Alex). Often on visits to other homes, restaurants, and the like, their comfort zone comes with them; for example, when Alex was two, he took my grandmother's antique hand mixer with us everywhere in order just to find comfort in the routine of the turning mechanism and those gears.

ALEX AS THE RED RANGER

Comfort Zones and repetitive activities bring linear, non-changing routine of security to those in which an abstract world can be painfully chaotic. Our son used to love doors when he was very little, and locks as they were predictable, the doors linear, and also a literal, or in the case of the dollhouse at his speech therapist's clinic, a figurative reminder of there is always an escape. These items of comfort—we still take "blankies" with us—remind those on the spectrum that while the outside world can be scary, if you bring a "friend," it can also be manageable. Our son wore weighted vests for years both in public, at appointments, and at school. He often still has a small koosh in his pocket or backpack to squeeze. Friends and family accept, understand, and know that Alex will always have an electronic with him (even almost completely deaf, he is no fan of loud sounds in crowded places).

Autism From Diagnosis to Adulthood: The Spectrum Journey

Since Alex was out of utero, it seems, after he got passed the staring at ceiling fans and *Baby Einstein* phase (I could leave him for hours in front of everything video *Baby Einstein*—I thought my baby and toddler was just really "good" when in actuality, he had autism . . . who knew?!); next, Alex moved toward the electronic stage; first: it was calculators. And when Alex was in his 2–3-year-old age at IPSEP (Infant Preschool Special Education Program) in our Plymouth-Canton School district that he began at age 19 months, his teacher held a yearlong nighttime, once a month program for parents, to help their child conquer one "behavior" that year. Ours was to be able to eat out in public at a restaurant with him, even just a McDonalds. His (and our) teacher asked what he was currently interested in outside of school, and we said "calculators," and she suggested a used Gameboy for him to get and try since he liked the predictability of "buttons" and "hand held electronics" and the rest is Alex history . . . accept your kids, embrace their interests . . . that helps to actually bring them out of their comfort zone worlds . . . and into ours . . .This program helped my husband and I so much! I hope that in a Covid world, these in person parent trainings can continue; albeit, I know of many good ones that are done online, and if you reach out to me at dawnhkspectrumjourney@gmail.com , I can help you find them.

Speaking of sensory issues and comfort zones, a few years ago at the gym, I headed to the corner nook, to stretch and reflect. I was carting weights, mat, water, phone, an exercise ball—a big one, for which I lost control, and it rolled to my surprise to an unexpected 20 something aged male, squeezing a koosh ball, sitting on a mat, wearing headphones, and watching a video—comfortable, cross legged in his sweats, and when I apologized to him for the interruption, he spoke to me, with eyes averted over my left shoulder, outlined dark circles I see often under my son's eyes, squeezed his koosh, and tried to say my interruption of his video was okay. Later, after this individual got up to move again to a private corner, I recognized his toe walking, and understood that in his way, he was enjoying the gym, being out in public, socializing, if in the margins. To give my evaluation of this individual some creed, I spent a past lifetime and three states ago as an early on evaluator for ages 0-3 to speech, language, developmental milestones—I was one of those individuals—with a notebook, some forms, and a case of toys, for whom your child was referred to for developmental delays. And because I'm proudly Alex's mom, I had no doubt that this man, at the gym, was on the autism spectrum.

Dawn Ham-Kucharski

In our case, with our Alex, sensory processing integration dysfunction complications from cerebral palsy, and especially autism, are caused, as we have learned from autopsies, from neurons that do not branch out appropriately (and can often regenerate, though, from early sensory integration therapy—play containers of beans, swings, deep pressure compression, brushing, and all of those OT tools). For Alex, now age 24, sensory integration is still a daily hurdle, part of our planning process to consider for any endeavor, and while he can now advocate more for himself in regard to this and knows what works to self-regulate, yet Alex can still get heightened anxiety leading to almost panic attacks from sensory issues—insert a few years ago when our local high school had outdoor band percussion, practice near the track where Alex's Special Olympics team was practicing—Alex was in pain—covering his ears, eager, at age 21, to get to me, to get off the track to give me the "Alex Autism Hug"—stand in front of me, bend his head over to rest his chin, eyes down, on my left shoulder—no actual arm contact—but his way of non-verbally saying "I'm a wreck", "I need my mom." Since we were at Special Olympics, before a panic attack could ensue, I was able to get him off of the track, walk him to our car gently while he covered his ears, face contorted in pain—one step away from crying and meltdown, and get him to his iPad to recoup. Thankfully, I was at Special Olympics, and we were surrounded by understanding and support from our friends who "get it." But I am still haunted by the memories of other adults in a Target, in a mall, making snide comments on how they would parent my child, and I am appreciative of others, strangers, who have offered kindness, assistance.

And the stares, the comments, do not change with age—Yes, I'm looking at you, ma'am, whom, a few years ago at our local Ihop, stared at my child as he calmly made his age 21 self through a crowded lobby area as we exited wearing headphones. Being me, I asked her if she had some questions for me regarding our son, she mumbled some excuse and looked away. If you are living this experience as an individual with autism or sensory integration processing disorders (There's no tags on my shirt and my food must never touch on the plate) or a caregiver to someone who falls in these categories, let me highly suggest Carol Kranowitz' *The Out of Sync Child.* You are not alone . . .

Also, awhile back, I went out for a late-night dinner with friends: the goal was to enjoy a meal together, at a venue where we could eat outside on a beautiful day, that was the restaurant feature my friends were most looking for as we chose a place—I had an additional feature in mind—a restaurant where I could successfully choose a

~ 22 ~

food item for takeout, that my son would eat. None of our seven friends present were at all shocked that for Alex, we got take-out grilled mango salmon with rice and beans, minus the mango, rice and beans, with fries instead, as anyone who knows Alex knows that he would, literally, eat salmon for all three meals every day. Individuals with autism are food sensitive or food selective or quite possibly both. Individuals with autism have sensory integration dysfunctions, particularly with dysfunctions of how their body responds to certain smells and feels—a tactile dysfunction. This can make visiting other homes (we pack a meal!) or dining out a logistical nightmare. My friends who know and love our son accept his food issues, but not everyone can be so understanding. For years, Alex would not eat red meat, but now loves it, yet he is no fan of the feel of pasta, and he prefers his food not to touch, unless of course it is pepperoni on pizza. Then add in those covid pandemic empty shelves of our kids' favorite foods or drinks, and for those on the spectrum, they often are very food selective as in the hypothetical "my child loves chicken nuggets but will only eat Tyson Dinosaur ones" food selective. I remember setting up a shelving unit in my husband's home office, where we stocked the favorite non-perishables that I would order in bulk on Amazon, especially our son's favorite Gatorade Zero drink flavors during Covid lockdown in 2020.

Many friends and family just feel that if you give an individual what they should eat, and tell them to, that the individual with autism will just eventually cry "food uncle" and suddenly manifest into a person eager to try new things and taste, but with their neurons that did not branch out, it is immensely difficult, due to the tactile dysfunction, to get an individual with autism to try new foods. For example, Alex detests warm cereal, the smell of popcorn makes him vomit-literally, and he is prone to not eat at all, unless it is something he knows he will like—he traveled by plane from Atlanta to Osaka Japan—a very long trip, only choosing, amongst actually really great airline options to only eat saltines and drink apple juice—the entire flight and ditto on the way home. And on the bright side, while still limited in food choices, I would say as he has gotten older, his food tastes have immensely grown. While Alex still prefers waffles, hard boiled eggs, pizza, chicken and the like, his tactile defenses have lowered their insurmountable walls, and he will try stuff—some he ends up liking—peanut butter sandwiches, grilled cheese sandwiches, turkey, steak, sushi, rice, teriyaki sauce, wasabi, BBQ chips and BBQ wings, raw broccoli (only raw—no dip!) and others he will not try again—insert chili. This is not our kids being rude—it is truly how their minds, bodies process the taste, smell, feel of the food—a sensory onslaught that often loses to something amazing—like hot fudge sundaes or root beer floats. The best thing you can do is have an OT who specializes in sensory integration therapy and helps to work through tactile activities with your child—fingerpainting, shaving cream, before even having some good old fashioned fingers play with peanut butter. In our case, I listen to my son—he is an adult, and I respect his food choices; we all enjoy a great meal that way.

BENTO BOX: ALEX'S LUNCH CONTAINER FOR HIS COLLEGE ON CAMPUS CLASS DAYS

Sometimes, we all eat repetitive foods—for Alex, on the same day—as in the day we made two different visits to McDonald's. Yes, you read that right. Two. It was end of semester crunch time, and with many appointments and much schoolwork, for both Alex and I, we were feeling the anxiety heightened. Alex's food comfort zone are those golden arches, and since at lunch time the shake machine was down, we hit up a different McDs for dinner—and ordered just shakes. Alex always gets the exact same thing: fries, McNuggets with barbecue sauce, and a vanilla shake. Yes, our son has tactile defensiveness—is he striking out physically? Not at all! (We super missed Drive-Thrus and Restaurants during Covid shut-down!) Besides the senses we usually speak of sight, hear, smell, touch, feel, we also have vestibular—how our body regulates and balances in the space around it; proprioceptive, the way we respond to movement and how we move; and tactile—how things feel. While oatmeal and macaroni and cheese are two of my favorites, Alex's sensory integration dysfunction can't stand the texture. Put it another way, we all have some tactile defensiveness—no tags on my shirts—and never ever make my cereal mushy with milk. And individuals with autism, because of that difference in neuronal development in the brain, literally can feel pain from different textures. Like me, my child cannot stand food touching on his plate—Thank you Bento Box! And we have gone through many brushing therapies and the like to work on this—to heal, so to speak—although I hate using that word—but for example, my child as a little boy, couldn't stand small grains—like sand—so we worked from playing in a container—literally sitting in it—full of red kidney beans, then added rice, then just rice, then rice and sand, and then sand.

Intervention with sensory integration therapy is the key—Alex can still become distressed when his tactile dysfunctions kick in, and that poor kid with those awful bulky hearing aids—literally the feel of those molds, and the way they rubbed, caused immense pain to distractions—his new light weight ones do not (And despite his profound hearing loss, Alex really never wears his hearing aids as an adult—his autism prefers things quiet) . If your child with autism seems out of sorts—Alex was a "highly energized" child with autism, and before he could talk, communication was expressed in his behavior—throwing things, crying, screaming, head banging (head boards, floors, cement driveways), and as communication developed, he could better indicate his needs, remember that listening to your child with autism is not just about hearing verbals, it is being able to read the non-verbals—we can now see when a possible meltdown is coming on, and know the triggers to avoid, but as you are still working through this phase with your loved one on the spectrum, remember that sensory integration dysfunction is literally a physical and cognitive cause—you cannot scream or punish one over something they have as much control over as any other individual with a chronic disease. The best phrase I was ever taught during Alex's early ASD years, came from Dr. Rick Solomon: "All behavior is communication," and when you can understand that you are on the steps to entering your child's world, and understanding, and they feel and know when you do, when you respect them. I'll toast my vanilla shake to that . . .

When Alex was diagnosed with autism, the first book I read was Temple Grandin's *Thinking in Pictures*. She illustrated for me the way Alex's mind works...a rolodex of images processed best when order is brought to their spinning. For Alex, the PECs (Picture Exchange Communication System) and Visual Schedule of photos in our home and in his classrooms, which initially teachers and we arranged for him, and as he became older, he helped to daily arrange, or even hand us to communicate, led to helping him find safety and focus in order and routine and independence and a feeling of control through visual learning and processing. Individuals with autism are extreme visual learners (and if you are a person who turns down the car radio when you are lost to concentrate, or love PowerPoints, you are a visual learner, too), and a few years back, as Alex was stressed over a term paper...a cultural identity memoir incorporating research on religion, family, peers, education, media, Alex said: "this is

ALEX IN SUMMER 2018 AT OTEMON GAKUIN UNIVERSITY IN OSAKA. HE WAS SUPPOSED TO ATTEND NANZAN UNIVERSITY IN JAPAN IN SUMMER 2022, BUT COVID DECIDED OTHERWISE, SO HE PARTICIPATED IN ZOOM ROUNDTABLES WITH NANZAN UNIVERSITY. AND IN DECEMBER 2022, HE COMPLETED AT PORTLAND STATE UNIVERSITY HIS BACHELOR OF ARTS IN INTERNATIONAL AND GLOBAL STUDIES ASIAN CONCENTRATION WITH JAPANESE LANGUAGE.

why I prefer biology, I can see my subject first, film it in my mind, and my report is created through mental visuals, not abstract summations". Even to this day, Alex keeps an emotional visual chart on our fridge to communicate how he is feeling. He only goes to movies whose story and characters he already knows (like *Star Wars* or *Jurassic Park*) because it stresses him out if he cannot visualize the story ahead of time. Alex did a lot of visual prep work before going to Japan to study in summer of 2018. The visual prep included *Amazon Prime* documentaries on Japan and our friends Jim and Misa for sharing their photo albums and workbooks of Japan and on culture with Alex before he headed to Osaka (Yes, our son studied abroad in Japan—without us—and yes, I would have never thought that a possibility when he was a child but believe in your child and yourself. See the inspiration from Holocaust Survivor Viktor Frankl https://www.youtube.com/watch?v=UgVA6nXCj1U). There are three learning styles educators learn to teach: auditory, kinesthetic (like group work, building things), and visual learners. Individuals with autism are the ultimate visual learner...

Resources

- **Comfort Zones** https://www.playproject.org/wp-content/uploads/2018/02/PrologueOrigins.pdf
- **Carol Kranowitz** *The Out of Sync Child* https://out-of-sync-child.com/
- **Sensory Integration Disorder and Therapy** https://www.iidc.indiana.edu/pages/sensory-integration-tips-to-consider https://iancommunity.org/cs/what_do_we_know/sensory_based_t herapies
- **Temple Grandin** *Thinking In Pictures* https://www.amazon.com/Thinking-Pictures-Expanded-Life-Autism/dp/0307275655
- **Autism and Food Sensitivities** http://www.shieldhealthcare.com/community/grow/2015/12/14/si x-reasons-children-with-autism-have-eating-issues/
- **Picture Exchange Communication System** https://www.nationalautismresources.com/the-picture-exchange-communication-system-pecs/
- **Visual Supports** https://www.autismspeaks.org/sites/default/files/2018-08/Visual%20Supports%20Tool%20Kit.pdf

References

Frankl, V. (2013). **Viktor Frankl & man's search for meaning.** *YouTube.* *https://www.youtube.com/watch?v=UgVA6nXCj1U*

Chapter 4 - Developmental Age

Some days, Alex is 24 years old. Sometimes 124. Sometimes a young child in many ways. The obstacles one often faces in public as the parent or caregiver of an individual with autism is that strangers, and even friends and family, can't "see" the disability. They see an almost 25-year-old and expect that age level of maturity and understanding to exude and permeate his identity. But parents and caregivers of those with autism know, that in all aspects of the individual with autism's being, it is not the biological age that one places expectations, goals, or even mood, educational, or social abilities to reflect, but rather the "developmental age" they are such as we see in the theories of Piaget and Erikson.

Erikson's Stages of Psychosocial Development

Approximate Age	Psycho Social Crisis
Infant - 18 months	Trust vs. Mistrust
18 months - 3 years	Autonomy vs. Shame & Doubt
3 - 5 years	Initiative vs. Guilt
5 - 13 years	Industry vs. Inferiority
13 - 21 years	Identity vs. Role Confusion
21 - 39 years	Intimacy vs. Isolation
40 - 65 years	Generativity vs. Stagnation
65 and older	Ego Integrity vs. Despair

Piaget's Theory

Stage	Age Range	Description
Sensorimotor	0-2 years	Coordination of senses with motor response, sensory curiosity about the world. Language used for demands and cataloguing. Object permanence developed
Preoperational	2-7 years	Symbolic thinking, use of proper syntax and grammar to express full concepts. Imagination and intuition are strong, but complex abstract thought still difficult. Conservation developed.
Concrete Operational	7-11 years	Concepts attached to concrete situations. Time, space, and quantity are understood and can be applied, but not as independent concepts
Formal Operations	11+	Theoretical, hypothetical, and counterfactual thinking. Abstract logic and reasoning. Strategy and planning become possible. Concepts learned in one context can be applied to another.

ERIKSON AND PIAGET

For example, Alex is almost 25, at least biologically, but developmentally Alex is more of a 19-year-old, and despite his outward appearance, his developmental age is where he is at emotionally; sleeps in late; can be super helpful or super emo; and at times, super anxious. We reach Alex better by recognizing that he is his developmental age—meeting his expectations there. But he, honestly, was also the athlete snuggling with his blankies at a Special Olympics event a four years ago—to have their comfort—like we see in children, yet to be able to giggle, bemused and proud, when being flirted with by a fellow athlete lady, or absolutely frightened by a yellow jacket he encountered outside. And until a few years ago, Alex wanted all of his Power Ranger action figures in a laundry basket next to his mancave chair "just to know they were nearby."

Alex still needs reassurance from his parents (don't we all!) and still looks to us for his comfort, his anchor, his safety. And while it may be hard for others to understand, even Alex has been able to communicate to us that he "often feels like a little child," or that he feels like he "floats between two worlds" . . . his biological age and where he is developmentally, and the world of neurotypicals who don't quite get him and his fellow Special Olympic Athletes who do. And I wonder, when I see his non-verbal friends, who I know have so much knowledge, so much to express with us, do they feel, as Alex once pointed out in a college response paper, that they "feel isolated from" their peers? I'm betting they do . . . and maybe, just maybe, if we met them at their developmental level, they wouldn't.

Often, from parents of neurotypical kids, we have heard how they understand what we go through, they were so busy when their children were at home, too. In this case, I appreciate and feel like they see and accept Alex's developmental stage, but these parents of neurotypical children, don't recognize the reality that so many parents of kids on the spectrum face, that in reality, that even as an adult, Alex, while sweet and kid like, will still need us to be his caregivers, even if he lives independently, to have us nearby, to take him to his appointments (a new hurdle in the Age of Covid when your child with ASD is an "adult" and either has to go into medical appointments solo or only with one caregiver), to his activities

ALEX AT THE TOLEDO MUSEUM OF ART: THE ART OF VIDEO GAMES IN 2014

, to grocery shop, to be his world, his comfort zone, and for us to remember that even when he is fifty, to see him at his developmental age—even if that means keeping those video games and systems since he began gaming at age three dusted and nearby, and those blankies clean . . .

Resources

- **Developmental Age vs Chronological Age**
https://aspiringyouth.net/developmental-vs-chronological-age-whats-the-difference/

References

Developmental Theories (n.d.). *Quizlet.*
https://quizlet.com/373391038/developmental-theories-diagram/

Chapter 5 - Social Skills

Friends, we all need to have them. Social development in individuals with autism is difficult, and vital to begin encouraging with early intervention, but the ability to make friends, tolerate all of the sensory and speech intricacies that go along with social navigation and building, and the confidence it ultimately builds, in all of us, can lead to success in all aspects of life for those with autism or any disability: visual, hearing, physical, cognitive, neurological, developmental, which many with autism also live with. There is a therapy for children with autism…it involves placing a child with autism in the middle of a room, a stage, and have them being rushed with neurotypical children who literally pull them into the play, and while we at Team HK (Our Ham-Kucharski family moniker) never went through that

ALEX AND HIS DAD AT A UNIVERSITY OF MICHIGAN DANCE MARATHON EVENT

protocol, we joined, when Alex was three or four, the University of Michigan Dance Marathon program (Go Blue!), a program that involves students raising funds for U of M Mott's Children's Hospital and Beaumont's Pediatric Rehabilitation Programs, while assigning a team of students to your child and family, and who take you out into the world, monthly, whether to a Chuck E. Cheese, Museum, a Bowling Alley, a Pizzeria or even their own apartments for a Transformers viewing party, all while volunteering at events the children attend like pumpkin carving parties, valentine's day dances, holiday parties, bike and martial arts therapies and summer camps, including tree climbing and co-piloting Cessna excursions for all the family members. From that early journey, we helped establish a Dance Marathon program at the University of North Texas in July of 2009 which supports the Children's Miracle Network of Cook's Children's Hospital in Fort Worth—just two weeks after moving to Texas, and two weeks before I was hired to teach at UNT by mere coincidence (Go Mean Green!). Alex also began playing baseball, soccer, and bowling with Miracle League of Frisco, Texas that same Fall (Baseball for all!), and with our move in January of 2011, he joined Special Olympics of Union County, New Jersey (Go Hawks) where he competed in swimming, and joined Paralympics of Union County—swimming, powerlifting and Pilates; a move back to Michigan, also 2011, got Alex as a member of Miracle League of Plymouth (Huge shout out to Debra Madonna for her grassroots of this phenomenal program that includes holiday activities, and bowling leagues and yoga), and our to Georgia in 2013 for within a month of moving to Forsyth County—Alex was playing baseball with Miracle League of Cumming (and golf!)—thank you Denny —and within two months of moving to Georgia in 2013, Alex was an athlete of Special Olympics Forsyth County—thank you Linda—and participating in social activities and an athlete on the swimming, bowling, equestrian, powerlifting, and track and field teams. In addition, at Portland State University, where Alex recently graduated from with a degree in International and Global Studies, Asian Studies focus with Japanese Language, he was included in a Kabuki production as a dancer and a Percussion musician. All of this took research, effort, paperwork, networking, and I recognize that in the Age of Covid, the ability to reach out to and participate in these types of programs became limited due to shut down and availability. But many if not all are back: Dance Marathon programs are at many universities nationwide in the United States (search your local ones!); as is Miracle League; and Special Olympics is an international program—search, search, search, search!

All these organizations became our family, included us in theirs, gave Alex physical activity (especially important for his cerebral palsy), gave him social skills, helped him to be a part of community that has strengthened and grown his confidence from early childhood into and through adulthood (he is almost 25!!!). Because of these organizations, their volunteers, we have friends for life who truly understand our journey, share great resources, and a kid who we were told would never talk (he does!); walk with only ambulatory assistance (a phenomenal lengthening surgery in 2012 and great recreational therapies leaves an adult stroller and wheel chair in our storage covered in spider webs); and a kid who until he was in 9th grade wasn't a diploma candidate, graduated high school with honors; was frequently recognized for his educational achievements at Georgia Gwinnett College; University of North Georgia; Portland State University and even traveled study abroad in 2018 at Otemon Gakuin University in Osaka for five weeks in

Japan earning straight A's in six credit hours of overseas education where because of culture and understanding, he was told not to share his need for the academic supports he receives in the States (Covid pandemic canceled a second study abroad in Japan at Nanzan University in 2020, albeit participated with that university in roundtables via Zoom in 2020). Thanks so much to those who have always cheered, encouraged, and included all of Team HK in these excellent programs, and to those of you with young children, teens, adults on the autism spectrum or with special needs—the most important thing they can be—is part of a community—and Dance Marathon Programs (throughout the country at many universities and colleges), and Miracle Leagues and Special Olympics provide all of these magnificent opportunities—"stand for the kids," "baseball for all," and most importantly: "let me win, but if I can't win, let me be brave in the attempt." Above all, even if Covid is keeping you or an individual with autism still home, there are so many great adaptive recreational groups and social groups participating in online Zoom gatherings.

STATE OF GEORGIA SPECIAL

OLYMPICS FALL GAMES, EQUESTRIAN

Resources

- **Living Learning Enrichment Center**
  https://www.livingandlearningcenter.org/cybersecurity-certification-program-for-adults-with-disabilities%ef%bb%bf/
- **Autism Speaks and Recreation**
  https://www.autismspeaks.org/activites-children-autism

Chapter 6 – Friends

One of the hardest things for parents and caregivers of children—whether young children or adult ones—is to see the world going on around us—without our kids included. Whether it is school parties, proms, social milestones, weddings, grandchildren, we see, at all developmental stages, times when our kids, no matter their age, just aren't included. We often will make our own "playdates"—I still am, and my son is almost 25. I'm blessed he has a friend in his life he is so close to now, whom he spent Saturdays with when we lived in Georgia and spends almost every Sunday gaming online with since we moved to Oregon, and he has cousins, his best friends, whom he online games with almost daily but since Alex was little, it was Rich and I coordinating Christmas in July parties at our home, video game parties, Halloween parties, to include all. Often, when Alex is with others, he will do what I still call "parallel play." He wants to be with others—on a past morning outing a few years ago, he noted how nice it was to be at Ihop and Walmart, even though he was doing exactly what he would be doing at home—on his iPad—but he was out, in public, with others. Alex is also, as of January 2023, working hard to get a job, but thus far, no bites yet, but he has applied to Graduate School, which will get him back in social and school activities with peers, but this down time, I am not going to lie, has been a struggle, since he graduated with his bachelor's degree. Our kids thrive on routine, and he's been in public school since age one, so I am working really hard each week for pragmatic and fun things for us to do together.

ALEX AND HIS COUSINS EVAN AND PRESTON KUCHARSKI

In Spring of 2019, my girlfriend Molly, a mom to a special needs son of her own, Jonathan, and a working mom, coordinated at her home an Easter party. She was warm, welcoming, a delicious array of autism sensory friendly snacks, snacks for parents, and she divided the party goers in half— as one set hid eggs, the other worked in her craft room on decorating plastic eggs and

ALEX AND HIS COUSINS EMMALINE AND CAROLINE HAM

filling them with candy for a local nursing home, and then that first crafting group looked for eggs, and then vice versa occurred—with the original crafters hiding eggs. Everyone enjoyed being in proximity with each other, playing games and doing crafts together, the moms bonding, and Alex was even introduced to *Pup Patrol*—and although he probably won't admit it—he really enjoyed watching it with a new younger friend. In addition, many of my friends of my husband and myself, have invited us to their homes for dinner often, and they always include Alex. Another friend, Jason, always made sure he included salmon for our salmon loving son when we lived in Georgia, even when Jason's made a completely different meal for the rest of us. I was so thrilled to have Alex invited to his friend Jonathan's house for the egg hunt referenced above. Alex talked about it all the next day, and rare, except with his friend Gavin (So much love and appreciation to his mom Linda), has he ever invited over to others' homes (Also Grateful to Alex's Aunts and Uncle and cousins who have had him stay with them in their homes, giving he and we mini vacations apart). Go ahead and invite Alex my friends, his friends—maybe he sits nearby the action with an electronic, but I guarantee, he loves being there. As will others on the spectrum—just go ahead and include them . . .

Resources

- **MAF (Make Authentic Friends) App via iTunes or Google Play for teens and adults on the autism spectrum**
  https://www.makingauthenticfriendships.com/

Chapter 7 - Dealing with Others

Autism Awareness, in April, is not just a month for those who have autism or love someone who does; rather, Autism Awareness is our everyday reality—365 days a year; seven days a week; 24 hours a day. The spectrum is a vast tunnel of multilayers—and every individual with autism is affected differently. Some are verbal, while others are non-verbal. Some are hypersensitive. Some are hyposensitive. Some are verbal. Some are echolalic. Some are non-verbal. The range goes from high functioning to low functioning and all points in-between (To be blatantly honest—I really, really despise the clinical terms of "high functioning" and "low functioning" and rare if ever use them—but clinicians and educators and caregivers often do, so here they are—my thoughts: everyone "brings something to the table!"). But no matter where the individual is on that autism scale, they are aware; their caregivers and parents are aware; and we all put in so much effort, that we can cry ourselves to sleep from exhaustion (if we get to sleep even—some with autism are up at all hours, and their caregivers have my heart and prayers—in our case, our son has borderline narcolepsy—idiopathic hypersomnia to be exact—so we have not had those very tough experiences of my friends' children who often never sleep . . . that's a whole other conversation), but no matter the effect of autism—they are all aware.

From our experience, one of the most painful things—separate from seeing your child reach so hard to a developmental milestone or as our heart breaks as they are not at peer levels in many facets of being, are the comments from strangers, the negative "we know how to parent your child even though we don't know you at all" kind of people, who are blazingly, blatantly willing in a matter of having spent a few minutes in your proximity at a store or a restaurant suddenly think they can help you "correct" your child on the spectrum's meltdown, and even continue to do so while you are calmingly trying to explain autism and the situation to them, all the while trying to rolodex in your mind and remember all of those handy techniques in deep pressure compression and the like that your child's therapists have taught you for this exact moment of meltdown when your child may be screaming, head banging, running away, biting you, hitting you, throwing things—and yes—Rich and I have experienced all these with our son.

 I am so appreciative of those individuals, strangers who when Alex was in full meltdown in a Target or a Meijers or a Wal-Mart who would genuinely care and try to help. Then there was the woman at Richardson's drugstore in Canton, Michigan. Alex was three and had an ear infection. We were both "spent" but the line was long, so I let him sit on my feet as we scooted our way toward the counter. The woman by me told me her thoughts on my parenting in no pleasant terms. I explained he was comfortable—I didn't mind him sitting on the floor wrapped around my feet (which he was doing calmly and quietly) and that he had autism and an ear infection. Then she told me she teaches kids with autism and that they "train them by the hand"— meaning corporeal punishment. As I was now 31, and standing in a pharmacy where all staff had known me since I was 6, I felt comfortable in back-up, and let this woman know I wanted the name of her school, her name, and was going to report her. She let up, yet still followed me to my car shaking her head in dismay. I would like to say this was the only time Alex and I experienced such treatment—but it wasn't. Whether when our son was non-verbal and eventually echolalic (like when he only spoke in phrases from Disney's *Dinosaur* "Stand Together" "Follow the

ALEX AND HIS POWER RANGER SUNGLASSES

Herd"—two of his favorites which he seemed to aptly apply in many situations), or when he went through a tactile sensory chewing phrase, or even summer of 2019 when I overheard grandparents at the Collection 's (an outdoor mall) in Cumming, GA, outside of Barnes and Noble dismayed at my son, an adult, wearing Power Ranger's sunglasses, or just a few years ago when a woman stared at my son at a crowded Ihop wait area that he walked through with headphones on staring at a YouTube on his iPad, so as to provide himself positive supports in a crowded situation. And the time when Alex's dad, Rich, almost punched an obstinate father at an Ann Arbor Michigan Mall whose son wouldn't stop purposely bullying Alex in a play area. And Rich is the calm yin to my hyper responsive yang….

And like I said, our kids know. Alex, as a student at Georgia Gwinnett College, had a great second biology group in his biology lab, but the first one wasn't, and his feelings were hurt. The first biology group ignored Alex in class (and he is brilliant in biology by the way), would only respond to each other, not Alex at all, on the group chat app. So, Alex told me that they were "avoiding him like the plague," and it is because he "is different." I made it a learning moment. Had him advocate for himself to his teacher—he got a fabulous new group, and the other folks pretty much disappeared from the class. But Alex can advocate for himself, and his parents are confident no matter the situation, but our feelings still get very hurt, too, and for those individuals with autism, who can't advocate for themselves—and for their parents, caregivers, and grandparents, I ask those who think they know better than we … to educate themselves … and shut up.

And this also happened once when I was out for lunch with a group of friends: an individual said to me: "Of course you can watch television, You don't have a job." Stunned (although knowing the person, not surprised), I responded that, "Yes, yes I do." And in reflection, I do not mean one I get paid for, say, an professor adjunct (my past gig for decades), but my real job, the 24/7 one 365 days a week, and while no monetary compensation is received, it sure comes with benefits, but also a lot of exhausting work: being Alex's mom. Having been a professor, undergraduate academic advisor, and copy editor, BA "Before Alex" and an at home parent full time, and a part time professor and an at home parent full time, at the same time, I feel entitled from within my vast experience to be able to say that being the at home parent full time of an individual with autism is way more work, time, energy, than any other "job" out there.

But strangely, I shouldn't have had to explain myself to this person at my lunch with friends, but out of some bizarre acceptance female guilt thing that made me feel small and meek, I responded that "the tv show I saw today was because my butt was up early at the gym," and while that was true, what if it wasn't? What if my son had been at school, at therapy, by some weird twist of fate somewhere without me along, and I was binging *The Incredible Mrs. Maisel* with a side of leftover cold pizza and a root beer at 2:00 p.m. on a weekday?—The moms, dads, caregivers of individuals with autism—we sure have earned a break—with double pepperoni—and if you understand me—you have walked in the same "Life with ASD" shoes . . . In almost 25 years of AA (After Alex), I never cease to be amazed at the amount of people, who think I have "all this time on my hands" . . . I know my friends with children with autism are feeling what I am saying . . .

Back in 2019, I also spent much of a past afternoon talking on the phone with a dear friend. That individual has two young sons (preschool age and elementary age) recently diagnosed with autism, and a third child—under age one. She has begun that awful experience of strangers commenting on her children with autism, and not in a helpful manner, and she is working the navigations of medical, educational, family, social complexities, times two kids, that comes with the Autism diagnosis. As she shared with me, I thought about how even, at that time of our phone chat, that 19 years later into Alex's diagnosis, I can still feel so small. Although not shocked, by a snide comment or a stare, and my friend, like me, is an at home parent, for whom others will often wonder "what she does with all of this 'free' time,"—as if! Her two children on the spectrum do not sleep well at night, and a baby—she loves all three with such passion and is eager to do and learn all that she can but is also in that early diagnosis phase of despair. I cried, laughed, swore with her this afternoon—she's a displaced Michigan girl like me—she in Alabama and at that time, I in Georgia—and I was more than honored to have her trust, and to curse the Fates and love her kids with her, all in that same one conversation.

And to those who ask us parents, caregivers of children with autism what do we do with all our free time you ask? There are multiple volumes of books, blogs, websites, articles, devoted to having a child with autism—let me bop you on the head with some . . .

Chapter 8 - Travel

Yes. We travel. A lot. From the moment my husband Rich and I began dating in 1989, we have been anything but sedentary, and when our three pound preemie Alex entered the world, we were eager to get him out and on the go—literally—the first place we took our now 4 lb. 11 ounce child when he was discharged at age 5 weeks from the NICU was straight to Plato's Coney Island Restaurant in Canton, Michigan for lunch with family and friends. Sure—we got looks . . .but it is now a great memory as just seven months later my father would pass away after 10 years of illness, and I'm grateful to friends, family, even my hairdresser, who kept Alex overnights for us, giving love to our baby, so we could spend hospice time with my dad, and post funeral time with family.

When Alex was 26 months of age, the autism diagnosis came, and we pictured a secluded child, in a literal and metaphorical corner, who might also be a savant pianist, as my only exposure to autism prior to that diagnosis was in 7th grade health class that showed a film on a blind autistic savant pianist—this Alex was not, and the day after his diagnosis, Alex and I headed on our already planned trip to my best friend Jhoanna Robledo in San Francisco, where I chased him laughing in and out of solitary confinement at Alcatraz—individuals with autism love anything linear—even Alcatraz—as lines, rows, are predictable.

ALEX AND I IN SAN FRANCISCO...TWO DAYS AFTER HIS AUTISM DIAGNOSIS. PHOTO CREDIT: S. JHOANNA ROBLEDO, MY BEST FRIEND

Since then, we have traveled often, and every time Alex soars—he first said "momma" on a cruise to Jamaica when he was three—the same island where a tour guide asked why he didn't talk, and

ALEX AT AGE 2 1/2 IN MEXICO

promptly lifted Alex on to his shoulders when we said Alex speaks with his hands, and with an enthusiastic "cool," the man lifted Alex into the air, for a ride of that beautiful island with a better view. Alex has been to Japan (solo--five weeks study abroad summer 2018), Canada, Mexico, Jamaica, The Bahamas, Grand Cayman, 38 states including Alaska, and has lived in five states: Michigan, Texas, New Jersey, Georgia, and Oregon—Alex even attended middle school in three different states (I figure if you can do that, you can do anything!). But even without travel from home, we are always on the go, and as parents and caregivers of those with autism know, routine is hard to break, especially for those on the spectrum, but just keep trying. It only took me from age two to five, to figure out when Alex would run away from me at the mall, and I would scream "don't run," that all he was hearing was "run" and follow my direction to the extreme. "Stop" works better. We do staycations. We plan an adventure each weekend—a recent was Depoe Bay, Oregon, and the weekend before was to the nearby Portland Japanese Garden. No doubt that Covid threw a wrench into all of our abilities to get out and travel, let alone just go eat in a Waffle House or a McDonalds, but thankfully, at least in the United States, as of the writing of this book, most places have reopened as has the ability to travel.

And I get it these travels, day trips, just going to a Target or Applebee's is not always easy. Alex is visual—wants to do what he knows—at this point, age almost 25, all of our vacations are still planned near an aquarium, a zoo, somewhere with animals and nature, and even if it is something he wants to do, he almost always asks what time we will leave said activity or adventure, but the growth we have seen from all of this, and the perspectives of the world he has gained, and his ability to maneuver in it, such as in Japan, without us, makes it all worth it.

Autism From Diagnosis to Adulthood: The Spectrum Journey

Don't give up—we've had some major meltdowns—Ellis Island circa 2005—Alex loved chasing the seagulls, and clearly expressed through meltdown witnessed by our tour group of mostly senior citizens that he was not ready to get back on the boat to leave back to Manhattan, but you know what: that was in the morning, and for the rest of the day, those folks talked on the bus to us about autism, what is it, so and so's grandchild has it, and offered help and offered lots of chips, crackers, and candy to a most happy Alex who regained sweetness when we hit the McDs in Times Square for lunch—autism and those golden arches go together . . . Happy travels!

Chapter 9 – Holidays

Every year, still, we put out cookies and milk for Santa and carrots for his reindeers and the Easter Bunny still hides eggs in our home to be found on Easter Sunday morn. Holidays, as joyous as they are, takes prep, planning, errands, shopping, house cleaning, and even us neurotypicals can become overwhelmed—now imagine being an individual with autism--who craves routine to navigate, regulate, even their typical days (I have that child who even before we go somewhere he wants to be, askes what time we will be home—like I said—craves routine—and schedules—and schedules of routine)—then add in trips, company, new smells, new sounds, new lights, new tastes, people they might not even know, time off from school, and the holidays can soon become a sensory minefield waiting to erupt into literal shutdowns and meltdowns. And throw off all of that with new traditions during the height of the Covid pandemic, and I know you all get it and get the picture…

When our son was a little one—okay—through his teens and onward, you can guarantee that October 31st to January 2nd, would illicit anxiety and nerves so gargantuan, that his anxiety would go: straight to his stomach and digestive system—we will leave out the rest of the details, that mysteriously heals after the last toast, round of "Auld Lang Syne," and after the Michigan Wolverines (hopefully!) win a New Year's Day bowl game! We have been blessed to have family and friends who have, for the most part understood, asked about, wanted to help make Alex feel comfortable with favorite foods, quiet areas and the like at holiday events, and understood his need to regulate with a Gameboy at a family dinner table, but not all have been so understanding, and they know who they are, so no need to mention—those I referred to here once told us when Alex was three, that if they "had Alex for a weekend, they could cure him of his autism". . . we stopped spending holidays with them for at least nine years after and probably should have stopped altogether).

ALEX WELCOMING THE END OF THE HOLIDAY SEASON 2010 AND ENJOYING A UNIVERSITY OF MICHIGAN FOOTBALL BOWL GAME

Autism From Diagnosis to Adulthood: The Spectrum Journey

Our kids with autism—at all holidays—the sensory overload is painful. My son, for example, once he began to talk—would switch prepositions—"off" meant "on"—as in the lights "off" meant that he wanted the "off lights" turned "on," and at a holiday dinner by candlelight only, he once ran his hand through every candelabra flame lit on the table when he was around age four or five, in the darkened room, screaming "lights off" and crying—for which then his stomach issues also kicked in. There are so many more, though, wonderful supportive stories, than negative, and my cousin Delores, who since long before I was born, hosts every Sunday before Christmas for my mom's maternal side of her family at her farm house, and when Alex was about five, Delores noticed Alex's need to have some calm, regulation time, in a crowded festive home, made him a picnic in one of her upstairs bedrooms, surrounded with toys that once belonged to her children and grandchildren and great-grandchildren,

tucked him into bed in cozy heavy blankets—Alex likes deep pressure— and had dinner plate brought up to him (he loved this—became a new tradition for a few years), while the rest of us, including the rest of the children cousins—ate in the kitchen and dining room. Alex loves his cousin Delores so much—because she has always accepted him, as have many of our family—on all sides. And as referenced in regard to so much, Covid had changed the gameplan on how we all experience holidays with family and friends, and I'm so grateful

ALEX AND OUR COUSIN DELORES ABOUT 13 OR 14 YEARS AGO AT CHRISTMAS TIME AT HER FARM

for all who are still with us and have always been there for Alex and us.

To prepare for holidays with kids on the spectrum, social stories work wonders, rehearsing what is to occur, showing family photos, talking ahead with family and friends to whom your child will interact, and honestly, we still often bring our own food for Alex and always his favorite electronics, and I'm grateful to our friends and family who accept and love Alex for who he is, and if your friends and family don't do the same with your child on the spectrum, guess what, you can just not go—why place unneeded stress on yourself, your child, your family? Saying no and not going can be hard—been there, done that, but we have, and if you need to, you should, too—say "no" and don't go—just don't be with those who bring negative energy to you and your child—there are so many of us—who love and accept them . . . you can bring them to our home . . .

TEAM HK THANKSGIVING 2022 TOAST

Chapter 10 – Toolbox

This section first came to me when I was totally going to write on another topic, but as those of us very aware of autism know, way too f**king well, plans can change. Autism is that pas de deux, that dance of two, knowing each other, finding our space, but instead of stillness glides of ballet slippers, emotionally, it is more like tap dancing with a loud marathon of shuffle ball changes on what can feel like thin ice . . . as parents of children with autism, whether your child is are age one or four or 14 or 24 or 64, we have to be ready to take the lead, when the tempo of life crescendos to a rapid pace that shatters routine and needs redirection. Thus was our day the day I went to write this section. Alex had a biology exam the next day for the lecture biology class—and he had the reviewed for two weeks—he had studied and studied and studied, and the next day looked to be one of those rare moments in the psychoeducational paradigm of anxieties that is school on the spectrum, where he just might not get close to full panic attack mode at the thought of the exam. We've worked on tricks—breathing for him, and I, like some prehistoric Easter bunny, hide stones with uplifting messages within the path of that exam location—and we were ready—and he calm—and then his teacher wrote his class today saying he had goofed on a schedule, and this goof was huge—he forgot that the next day was also the Biology Dept "common practicum" for the lab courses, and the students must review all lab assignments from the semester; be able to label everything known to biology scientist kind—by tomorrow morn at 8 am, without a review sheet, three hours before they were to take their lecture class exam two on multiple chapters. Both tests would be an hour and 45 minutes long. When I received the panic text from Alex around noon, I remembered who I was, my most important role: Alex's mom. I briefly stewed, called my husband and swore—not at him—but just to get it out, and got down to business. I asked Alex if he wanted to speak to the Dean of Science and Technology, I knew what my choice would be, and Alex chose the opposite—he liked his professor, and the professor always was super available by his personal cell, and Alex has learned much from him in their work in the school garden, so Alex chose to tough it up, do the studying, come what may...so my job...was to prepare for the "come what may."

Dawn Ham-Kucharski

This is the point to young parents of children with autism to note that they should start making that "emergency mental toolbox", for when the dance of parenthood and autism seems to start to get super clumsy, and mental tripping and stepping on toes could begin. I suggested to Alex that we review together. If he would share his lab stuff, I could help home organize, but that the most important step was that we first must: CARB LOAD—you know—like runners the night before a big race. And we would carb load—if he could remain calm tonight as we reviewed together. Yes, I know, I bribed my son with pizza—but it is in my "emergency mental toolbox" and remember those days of PLAY Project, DIR, ABA—if we don't make it fun for our kids—they aren't going to do it—especially if it breaks routine—which is their comfort zone. (And goodness knows that during Covid shutdown, our routines were all broken and we all needed "comfort zones!") At least this time, regarding that biology unexpected review, I had a few hours heads up (that will so often not be the case!) So yeah, I bribed my son, and he taught me—the proper way to say all the biology lab terms that I still have no clue how to pronounce—but I am beyond proud that he does. I also know our kids—even when they are adults—are super visual, so for things like labeling microscopes and frog anatomy and guts, I used Alex's lab charts to copy, cut out names, cross out names with Scripto markers and created a matching game called "Three Times the Charm" and when he had them perfect three times—he was done—finally- after our four hours of gorging pizza—and even— laughing. And while our tap shoes were replaced with tranquil pirouettes by the end

of the eve—Alex still retreated up to his mancave muttering "I'm so f**ked" (he's from Michigan after all—cursing is our vernacular), but he said it with a smile, and calmly. Afterwards, I could hear him upstairs comforting himself with script play of *Mighty Morphin Power Rangers* . . . And that my friends calls for a standing ovation . . .

UNEXPECTED BIOLOGY TEST: BRING ON THE CARB LOAD FROM THE "TOOL BOX"

Resources

- **Pizza. Any Pizza…**

Chapter 11 - Education (oh the acronyms!)

During Alex's final weeks leading to graduation at Portland State University in November of 2022, I couldn't help but reflect on the phenomenal education he has received in five states that all deserve the designation of "Great": Michigan, Texas, New Jersey, Georgia., and Oregon. Alex began receiving services under an IFSP (Individual Family Service Plan) when he was 19 months of age for developmental delay and speech and language impaired, through our Plymouth-Canton School's Early On (0-3) program. We were new, and navigating the evaluations, therapies (at home, school, and clinical), along with classroom placement—pre-primary impaired--was made easier—and with less tears albeit some, thanks to the staff at the Tanger School IPSEP (Infant Preschool Special Education Program [so many acronyms!]).

At age 25 months, Alex's teacher Joyce called me and asked if we would be a part of an experimental program that Fall—there were similar Alexes in the pre-primary impaired classroom in the Plymouth-Canton School District, and she wanted to do a special self-contained class the next school year of that seven—in that 2001-2002 school year, six of the seven, including our son, would be diagnosed with autism spectrum disorder.

ALEX AT TANGER SCHOOL IPSEP (INFANT PRESCHOOL SPECIAL EDUCATION PROGRAM) IN PLYMOUTH MICHIGAN

At age 3 came our first IEP (Individualized Education Plan), and Alex would remain, rightfully so, in a self-contained classroom setting, in three states: Michigan, Texas, New Jersey, and included as possible: math, science, in mainstream general education classrooms as he got older. For the "Alexisms": multiple diagnoses with autism ruling the roost followed by hard of hearing / deaf , and cerebral palsy, a self-contained classroom—branched out into team taught, resource room, and inclusion throughout high school in Michigan and Georgia (yay for German and Technology classes!), and Alex would carry his IEP , neuropsychological evaluations from Michigan, Texas, New Jersey, and Georgia, with him to his placements as we moved or he advanced, and onto post-secondary at Georgia Gwinnett College (During his first year, except for Art Appreciation and Composition I, all courses were "Developmental" and non-degree credit, but they were so worth it in college study skills, college reading, college writing, and college math), University of North Georgia, and Portland State University—his supports lessened yet still used: copies of notes, recording and dictation of notes, extended test time, testing at the Disability Office, placement in front row with left ear to the professor, and early registration, following him even to university in Japan—where he actually chose to use none of his supports.

I'll be honest, I hear a lot of complaints about educators, educational administrators, and school staff (general and special education) from parents and caregivers, (even during Covid when school staff and educators and administrators had to rethink—on a few days' notice, the entire educational process!) and in our experience, I count three teachers (one in elementary, one in high school, one in college) who just had no interest in adhering to the IEP or respecting IDEA (Individuals with Disabilities Education Act) or college Disability Office supports. Rich and I, and now Alex, have always felt included as part of the IEP team, and have always found his teachers and school staff to be much more knowledgeable than us in knowing what he needed placement, supports, services wise at school than we. They were and are the experts. They challenge Alex while supporting him (they have challenged and supported us, too). The formula though, I think, for having made this work, in four school districts and three colleges no less, is respect—our respect toward them and understanding that our son is one of many on their student caseloads, not attacking them, and prior to every IFSP, IEP, College Disability Director Meeting (which Alex now handles solo), emailing at least two weeks ahead of time to the entire educational team, what we or he hopes to accomplish at the meeting: what supports we want, where we see him educationally, and getting their input. Don't just walk into any IEP or the like without having done so—if that is the case, you are a big part of whatever stalemate is about to occur and frustrate you all at the meeting. I personally want to thank everyone of Alex's educational staff—they rolled with the Alexisms, put up with his parents, and they are the reason Alex has graduated from college. Give respect toward all on the IEP team, and the same will come back to you, and your child will soar!

Resources

- **Special Education Acronyms Explained**
  https://dredf.org/special-education/special-education-resources/special-education-acronyms-and-glossary/

ALEX COVERED IN FOUR TERMS OF HIS UNIVERSITY LEVEL JAPANESE STUDIES UPON COMPLETION OF HIS LANGUAGE DEGREE REQUIREMENT.

Chapter 12 – Transition

In Spring of 2019, as I was dropping off my son at his college campus, a Dockers pants and polo shirt wearing professor, whom I did not know, tapped on my truck's window. He introduced himself as the Dean of the Physical Sciences Dept at Georgia Gwinnett College, and my son's Choices for Life Professor. Alex sat on the seat next to me wide eyed. The professor, Dr. Horowitz, said he wanted me to know that Alex was one of the best students he has had—polite and engaged and obviously keeping up with his reading and homework based on his class participation and exam grades. To say that I was proud would be an understatement (Alex said he was surprised to receive such a compliment), and just as when Alex was in Japan studying in 2018, where his professors here in the States had told him not to share his need for supports for his disabilities: "They won't know what to do with that over there," Alex was being seen both by Dr. Horowitz and his professors in Japan, as an individual, not a diagnosis (The Alexisms are: hard of hearing / deaf; cerebral palsy; autism; idiopathic hypersomnia; duplicate 8P23 chromosome; Large vestibular Aqueduct Syndrome; Anomaly sixth lumbar; torticollis; and the like).

When Alex was as young as four, in Michigan, we did Person Centered Planning (PCP) in Wayne County (like a county IEP [Individualized Education Plan]), a process developed at The Center for Self Determination. The trend in 2002, was to see the individual—with Person First Language—"My son has autism" rather than "My son is autistic." I liked and still like Person First Language: Alex might be diagnosed with A, B, C, but he is also an individual highly devoted to school who competes in equestrian and power lifting, and loves to study culture and to peacefully demonstrate and stand up for what is right. In 2019, and onward, I see a new trend to "Identity First Language"—I am autistic. I am deaf. I am physically disabled, to recognize that these diagnoses are a part of what makes up this awesome person, and I get it (see this great video here for illustration [and inspiration!]) on this topic: "Disabled Person or Person with a Disability" (Elainey, 2016) https://www.youtube.com/watch?v=SMKKze48Qbo "Identity" seems to be, and in many cases rightly so, the new buzzword. I need much more research, and I would love to hear all of your thoughts on this, but I also see "Identity First Language" as acceptance. There will always be dichotomic discourse in all communities—there used to be a push to "cure" autism versus "living" with autism. In the deaf and hard of hearing communities—there is "Deaf Culture" versus "Amplification." Both are right—if they suit the individual.

THE CHOICE OF WHO YOU ARE IS YOUR JOURNEY

So, my heart and mind, still feel "Person First Language" fits our son best, but maybe not yours . . . and that is equally okay!

I would love to hear the discourse on this—as a woman whose mom life has been around a vast amount of signifying terms "Idiopathic hypersomnia" per se (Google it) and whose whole career from tutor to copy editor to professor has been centered around language and its impact in the written word; I am interested in pushing diagnoses or disabilities to the margin and seeing the individual at the center, but I also know that for many disabilities that "can't be seen", like autism, that if the disability or diagnosis is recognized as the center, as part of the individual's identity, there can be great education to others, and understanding from others as well . . . thoughts? Let me "hear" them at dawnhkspectrumjourney@gmail.com

Resources

- **Person Centered Planning** https://arcmi.org/wp-content/uploads/sites/15/2017/03/How_Person-Centered_Planning_Works_for_You_367101_7.pdf
- **Center for Self Determination** https://www.self-determination.com/

References

Elainey, A. (2016, November 22). Disabled person or person with a disability?. YouTube. https://www.youtube.com/watch?v=SMKKze48Qbo

Chapter 13 – Medical

In 2019 as Alex finished up final exams, and per his usual physical response to anxiety and stressors, he developed a fever and his stomach was in knots and his normally tight joints became achier than usual, and his legs were tight, and knees swollen. Alex's physicality will react tenfold to the anxieties brought on to him by his autism, and those past few weeks saw this escalate to whole new levels.

What many do not realize is the physical toll autism takes on the individual with autism spectrum disorder. As parents and caregivers can surely tell you, from diagnosis through adulthood, you will have many on your child's team—teachers, respite providers, coaches, social workers, therapists, but you will also need a slew of medical folks: a primary care provider you trust immensely, and a team of specialists. Alex has overlapping diagnoses with his autism, but many of my friends' children with autism, see similar doctors and specialists, as autism literally can affect you from the brain to your heel cords.

Since Alex's ASD diagnosis at 26 months of age, he has seen the following medical specialists, and I will explain, in each listing, their purpose on being on your child with autism's team:

EEG. ALEX, AGE 10

- **Primary Care Physician—** Pediatrician or Adult: It was Dr. Terrance Murphy in 2000, during Alex's 24 month well check, who pulled from his coat pocket a brochure for Early On in the Plymouth Canton schools, and made Alex a referral to a developmental pediatrician, Dr. Richard Solomon, as Dr. Murphy told me there was something going on with Alex besides just his hearing loss.
- Next up was Dr. Richard Solomon—**developmental and behavioral pediatrician** who diagnosed Alex at 26 months of age

with moderate to severe autism and began intense early intervention with him.

- Our team has also included an **audiologist**—not just for hearing loss, but many of our children and adults with autism have central processing disorder—for sounds, speech, processing of speech, cognition—took us two years of Alex running away from us from sensory overload at the mall to say "Stop," which he promptly did. The two years prior, we would yell: "Don't run!" and all he would hear was "run"—so he did.

- A **gastroenterologist**—many kids on the spectrum—from control issues, from diseases of the gut, from anxiety, have digestive disorders—Alex has GERD and an emptying disorder where he only digests 30% of what he eats—constipation, diarrhea, leakage—all of the above—trust me caregivers and individuals with autism: you are not alone on this one

- He also saw a **psychiatric nurse** who helped with issues of potty training—urination, bowel—by age 6, Alex accomplished number one—literally, and by age 12—number 2—if your children or adults with autism have these issues—once again: you are not alone.

- Alex has been seen by **psychiatrists** on and off his whole life for anxiety, depression, and medication (not currently on, but in the past, Prozac worked well for him—currently whole food diet or close to it, and vitamins work better for him—he takes a multivitamin, fish oil, vitamin e, vitamin d, vitamin c, folate, zinc, calcium, biotin, probiotic, and echinacea—but all done in conjunction with his medical doctors and not just for autism—consult with your child's specialists) to help with this as well as therapy with psychologists and social workers.

- A **neurologist**—who can also diagnose autism, provide medications, Tourette's (which Alex and many children on the spectrum are diagnosed with at some point) and help with autism related seizure disorders after as individuals with ASD, after age 13, have a 26% chance of developing seizure disorders as compared to children without autism—of which only 1% develop seizure disorders after age 13 (Autism Research Institute, 2021)

- There are also **neurologists who specialize in sleep disorders**—many children on the spectrum do not sleep—we are opposite there—Alex has idiopathic hypersomnia borderline narcolepsy (he's a professional sleeper)—he sees a neurologist for, but the majority of those with autism DO NOT SLEEP.
- Alex also, on and off, sees a **genetic specialist**, and continues to do so. Many individuals with autism have related genetic disorders—like Fragile X—and as tests and science become more precise—we know—based on rates of siblings with autism, there is a genetic component. Alex has a rare duplicate 8P23 chromosomal disorder, and also sees a cancer genetic specialist in regard to his precancerous skin issues and precancerous colon polyps, but I know more autism genetics research will shed light in our children's lifetimes.
- Alex also sees a **physiatrist (physical medicine specialist)** and an **orthopedist**—Alex has cerebral palsy and autism—something people with either or both of those conditions do is walk on their toes—one from leg tightness (CP) the other due to sensory issues (autism)—both can lead to intense tight heel cords and hamstrings—which can be helped with PT, Botox injections, and bilateral lengthening's—we do all of the above.
- An **orthotist**—another component can help with shoe inserts, orthotics, ankle and leg braces, that can help with the toe walking of autism.
- A specialist of **Diagnostic Medicine**—like Dr. House from the television show *House*. Our son was referred to such a specialist at Children's Hospital of Philadelphia (CHOP)—many kids with autism have multiple diagnoses—a diagnostician helps you to coordinate, organize, and treat your child with autism, and coordinates the team of specialists.
- A **cardiologist**—our children can really stress their own hearts, or psychiatric meds can affect not only your liver, but your cholesterol levels, your arteries—Alex has a rare duplicate superior vena cava that floods his coronary sinus with too much fluid and a bundle branch blockage in his heart—we make sure autism doesn't physically creep up to worsen all of this.

- You probably also want an **allergist** on the team and a **dermatologist**—many children and adults with autism have food allergies and intolerances (Alex can't process fructose). They also have many other allergies and sensitivities. And Alex has eczema and psoriasis. Both of which are much easier to help take care of now that he is an adult.

- Alex has been seen by a **rheumatologist** to check for autism related autoimmune disorders.

- In addition, many individuals find great success with a doctor who thinks **holistically or is a naturopath**—I'm looking at you Dr. Susan Youngs—who will find alternative approaches to autism—she introduced us to probiotics and fish oil, amongst many other helpful things. Alex began at a young age seeing **chiropractors, salt room therapy, and massage therapists** (anxiety adds to tightening of his muscles issues) and as an adult he has begun seeing **Chinese Medicine specialists** and getting acupuncture.

- Alex also gets treated by an **ophthalmologist** for sensitivity to light, tracking visual issues, and did vision therapy in New Jersey—many individuals with autism have visual processing issues—Alex has better than 20/20 vision, but still has other visual conditions.

- And Alex still sees periodically **physical, speech, and occupational therapists**. Speech therapy for expressive speech delay; physical therapy for tight heel cords; and occupational therapists for sensory integration therapy, for which when he began at age two, really helped Alex's speech to develop once he would work on his sensory integration dysfunction issues. Many speech therapists, physical therapists and occupational therapists are also working at **therapeutic horseback riding and hippotherapy centers.**

- Finally, throughout life, individuals on the spectrum need a great **dentist.** Alex had sensory issues as a young child with dental cleaning, then we met a pediatric dentist, when Alex was three, who used "papoose-ing" , like a cozy cocoon for which Alex liked the deep pressure input, while wearing sunglasses to protect his sensory responses from the dental lights, and before long, Alex, like a butterfly, no longer needed that cocoon, and since he was preschool age, has loved getting his teeth cleaned—also getting the

Play-Doh dentist set help, and letting Alex pretend to "clean our teeth". A good occupational therapist can also recommend the right toothbrushes and sensory tools to get those with autism used to dental cleanings. We discovered at the age of 15, also from a fantastic dentist that Alex had six wisdom teeth, and he referred us to a very kind oral surgeon. Finally, even at the age of 24, Alex just got braces, and he has been blessed with not only a great orthodontist, but one who's sister is the hygienist for another kind dentist near by. How awesome is that! Dental health is so important for physical health!

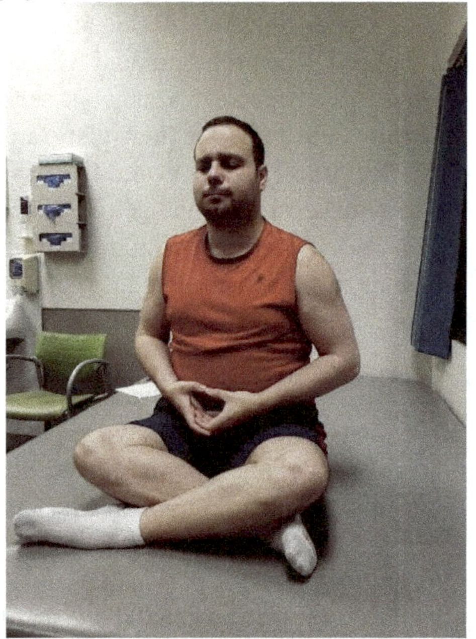

ALEX GETTING HIS CALMNESS ON AT PHYSICAL THERAPY AT CHILDREN'S HOSPITAL OF ATLANTA, 2019

Remember, if your gut instinct questions the actions of a medical professional 90% of the time, your gut instinct is right, whether you are the caregiver or the individual with autism. We have had some "come to Jesus" moments with some professionals—Alex has, too. But don't give up—read online reviews, ask friends and families for referrals. Call your insurance provider—they often have online reviews within their own portals. Essentially, all of this keeps us on our toes, but also helps to have Alex feel his best, be his best, which helps his issues from his autism. Dr. Solomon once told me "all behavior is communication"—if your child is acting out—there may be a physical component going on. We usually know when Alex is about to be ill—as his behaviors will suddenly go haywire . . .

Resources (Some of Our Favorites)

- **Alliance Health and Wellness Center** http://www.drbonez.com/
- **Atlanta Rehabilitation and Performance Center** https://atlantarehab.com/
- **Blyss Chiropractic** http://drblyss.com/
- **Dawson Oral and Maxillofacial Surgery** https://www.dawsonoms.com/
- **CHOP (Children's Hospital of Philadelphia) Patrick S. Pasquariello Jr. Diagnostic and Complex Care Center** https://www.chop.edu/centers-programs/diagnostic-and-complex-care-center
- **Dr. Colin Walters** https://gradydentalcare.com/meet-the-doctors/
- **Dr. Susan Youngs Center for Exceptional Families** https://www.beaumont.org/services/childrens/childhood-development-disorders/center-for-exceptional-families
- **Gingell Chiropractic** https://www.gingellchiropractic.com/
- **Golick Pediatric Dental Associates** https://golnickpediatricdentistry.com/?utm_source=GMB&utm_me dium=organic&utm_campaign=Taylor
- **Hippotherapy** https://www.americanhippotherapyassociation.org/what-is-hippotherapy
- **One Mind Massage** https://www.onemindpdx.com/
- **Pham Dental Care** https://phamdentalcare.com/
- **Reese Orthodontics** https://reeseorthopdx.com/
- **Salt Med Spa Halotherapy** https://saltmedspa.com/Dawsonville/

- **Therapeutic Riding** https://pathintl.org/programs/therapeutic-adaptive-horsemanship/
- **Village Wellness Center** https://www.facebook.com/profile.php?id=100024665091066
- **Vitalize Acupuncture** https://www.vitalizeacupuncture.com/meet-us

References

Autism and seizures (2021). Autism Research Institute. https://www.autism.org/autism-and-seizures/

Rosen, T. E., Mazefsky, C. A., Vasa, R. A., & Lerner, M. D. (2018). Co-occurring psychiatric conditions in autism spectrum disorder. International Review of Psychiatry, 30(1), 40–61. https://doi.org/10.1080/09540261.2018.1450229

Chapter 14 - Depression, Anxiety, Medications, and Suicide

A few years ago, while feeling completely overwhelmed by test anxiety, final projects, and final exams, Alex, tired and frustrated with expressive speech issues and physical disabilities, and social isolation ("my science group members avoid me like the plague" he wrote early in this semester to his professor) said: "I should have died before I was ever born." While biologically, at that time, Alex was almost 21 years old, developmentally, he was in those teen angst years, like a 15-year-old or 16-year-old, and his emotions can take those mid teen bends and turns. But depression and anxiety have been a constant battle for him, such as it is for many children and adults with autism spectrum disorder, and quite honestly, while we listened to him, got him to the gym, discussed anxiety strategies—he likes the woods—so take a stress break as needed to our screen room that looked into the Appalachian foothills; he loves animals, so I suggested at heights of anxiety, at least at home, to take a break to snuggle with his dog Biscuit—; use his meditative pillow to sit and do some breathing exercises.

PHOTO OF A ZEN GARDEN AT A TEMPLE IN KYOTO WHERE ALEX PRACTICED MEDITATION. PHOTO COURTESY: ALEX HAM-KUCHARSKI

For some years now, Alex has been at a developmental stage where he recognizes differences now in himself and others whether it be speech, physical disabilities, isolation, social awkwardness, relationships—couples, dating, and we feel that we must be willing to recognize what he is telling us, and reiterate what he says to us, so we show him we are being active and caring listeners, provide a hug, a back rub, and then when his anxiety has lowered, talk strategy.

As a young child, depression could hit Alex in huge waves. And as we have unfortunately seen, and lost some of his friends to, for those with autism, suicide occurs on way too frequent of a basis especially in the teen biological and developmental years. Since age seven, Alex has seen both psychologists, therapists, social workers, and psychiatrists—the best in Michigan—the worst in Texas—who so over drugged him with medications for mental diagnoses he does not have—such as schizophrenia and had him on such high doses of everything else, that we literally moved to New Jersey to get away from their archaic psychiatric protocols, and were blessed to receive services at CHOP (Children's Hospital of Philadelphia) that took six months to successfully ween him off of all medication that Texas had put him on. Except for this time with CHOP, Alex has been on a low dose of Prozac, since age seven, when he would literally spend half of his school day dismantling a classroom from anxiety, and dismantle his bedroom as well, and when Rich and I were separated in 2012, Alex resumed 10 milligrams of Prozac, and that seems to have thus far been his needed level when he has been on it. In 2021, and under medical care, he was weaned off Prozac and has remained that way since, and once again, under medical care, he is instead using magnesium and echinacea. Remember, you must not make any medical choices unless in consultation with your loved ones with autism's medical specialists and primary care physician.

We have to listen to our kids—Alex has told us deep honest things: thoughts of actions, fears, concerns, that we, no matter how hard, have had to let him know we are listening, will provide resources and support for, and love him always. The reality of autism is the reality of everyone who suffers from depression disorders— you must not tell someone to "just get over it." That is not engaged communication—that is disheartening and cruel. Many of my friends' children with autism have been hospitalized, repeatedly, with mental health concerns and depression, and as I said, some lost their lives to their depths of despair, and I cannot begin to fathom what their parents and caregivers have been through, experience every day . . . but I do want to honestly bring up this conversation of depression, anxiety, hospitalizations, suicide that in society, even in 2023, is so taboo—mental health disorders are a serious biologically originated condition, and as parents and caregivers of individuals with autism, the daily living with such symptoms of autism is a constant vigilance, exhausting, a parental heartbreaker of enormous proportions, and in this book, it would be negligent of me to not make the reader aware of facets of the disorder, including its high ranks of psychiatric conditions and rates of suicide: "A growing number of research studies have found that autistic youth and adults appear to have higher rates of suicidal thoughts, plans, or behaviors than other people do. As a group, their suicide risk may be two to seven times higher than the risk for youth and adults who do not have autism" (Sarris, 2022). Suicide has even higher prevalence amongst individuals with autism who have family history of mental illness and / or suicide. And we know all of these has multiplied in the age of covid. In Alex's family, he lost a paternal great-grandfather and his maternal grandmother to suicide. His dad and I live with this in our concerns for our son's well being every day. And I know many of you reading this, fall into these same areas of concern for yourselves and your loved ones, too.

Resources

- **ASERT: Bringing Autism Resources Together**
  https://paautism.org/resource/be-well-think-well-suicide/
- **Crisis Supports for the Autism Community**
  https://sprc.org/sites/default/files/resource-program/Autism%20Crisis%20Supports.pdf

References

Sarris, M. (2022, September 7). Autism and the troubling risk of suicide. Spark. https://sparkforautism.org/discover_article/autism-suicide-risk/

Chapter 15 - Individuals with Autism Dealing with Grief

A five years ago, a close girlfriend of mine in Canton, Michigan died. She courageously battled in much pain, for years, the insidious of cancer that just kept eating at her. We met somehow in the early 2000s—it is hard to remember how because it just seems like she was always in my life. Both of our sons have autism, and we're from the same hometown in Michigan. I am guessing we met at either a Wayne County support group, or the Ladies Night Out at Applebee's that I used to monthly facilitate (that she frequently attended), or via back in the day of yahoo listservs. All I know is that we became close—as did our boys when they were little, and she also has two other children—daughters, and her children have seizure disorders. She was also now a grandma and had spent her life with her true love by her side.

 But what I remember about my girlfriend, are those cold Michigan arctic tundra way below zero real temps winter nights we would meet, once a week, covered head to toe in our winter gear, along with our kiddos, and other girlfriends and their special needs kids at the Canton, MI Michigan Ave / Canton Center Road McDs—dragging in frozen slush behind us—unraveling our multilayer selves and our kids for affordable meals—a chance to sit and talk---and let our child autism posse work off that frigid stuck indoor winter angst in those play places. We became sisters over Cokes, fries and dollar double cheeseburgers . . . and she never had it easy—her husband and she struggled financially in blue collar Michigan, living in a local trailer park, and I never, ever heard her complain—and she had every right to—a full plate of school and doctors' appointments—but she was always a big dimpled grin, and she so loved her kids and her dad and her posse of pets, but especially her husband. She set the example for how to fight adversity with her #FuckCancer and #KickingCancersAss gear.

And while I was saddened to lose another close to my heart girlfriend to this disease (and my dad, and my grandpa, and my uncle, and my best friend), I am thinking about Jannie's children, and her son, and how individuals with autism grieve. I know for many of us, Jannie's reality for the many years that she fought cancer, is what about our children on the spectrum, when they lose someone, they love? And for our children on the spectrum, who are non-verbal, how do they express their grief, go through that process that for us "neurotypicals" can seem so overwhelming?

Our son has seen therapists on and off since he was a little boy; even voluntarily took himself to a campus health center psychologist last Fall, and Rich and I feel that therapy is an important part of wellness, but I have also seen the suicidal depths of our son's despair over losing his dogs, Daisy when he was 12, and his other dog, Tiffany, when he was 14. And I know Alex talks up at the stars nightly to both his great-grandma he had till almost age five, and his Grandpa Jim, whom he lost at age seven months but who left him a gift of a beautiful note and card—still on Alex's desk. Alex has since then had two hard losses: the first my best friend Jho to cancer in 2017, and the other, my mom, Dorothy Ham, to suicide in 2020. When Jho passed away in July of 2017, my goal was to go solo to the funeral—take my own ride with my own thoughts, feelings, music and drive from Atlanta to NYC to be allowed to feel my grief without having to care for others along the way—especially my son—as I had no idea how he would respond, and even on a regular day, he can usurp my energy, but he surprised me. Alex insisted on coming with me to his Auntie Jho's funeral to "take care of you mom." And you know what, he did. We drove to Virginia. Stayed with a girlfriend, and the next very early morning, picked up a college friend outside of DC, and Alex, my friend, and I rode the rest of the way to NYC together. And while Alex was so sad, he did take care of me. When I was the one sobbing out of control at the funeral mass, his hand was on my shoulder—his head on my shoulder, giving comfort. To this day, whenever a "phenomenon" occurs where we live, Alex will just say "awe mom, it is Auntie Jho just pulling one of her tricks" (her favorite day was April Fools—and her tricks and jokes were the best!).

So how will Alex respond to loss of loved ones in the future—his dad, myself, I don't know. I truly don't. My mom, Dorothy, was his best friend, and he was personally hurt by her purposeful overdose, but my mom had suffered from bipolar, depression, schizophrenia, multiple personality disorder her whole life since an early childhood of abuse in foster care before my incredible grandparents adopted her, and Alex knew of her struggles with mental health, but, honestly, she was also the person whom we trusted Alex most with. She understood better than any of us what living with neurodiversity is like, and they were close buddies who traveled together, played games together, hung out together. Alex can now speak of good memories with my mom three years after her suicide, but it took time for him to grieve and find acceptance. But if your loved one on the spectrum has a loved one, a friend, someone in their community, pass away, I know all individuals on the spectrum feel—just as much if not more than any of us, even if they can't express it. The *Autism Alliance* (2023) gives great advice:

- Don't expect a person on the autism spectrum to demonstrate their grief in the same way as other people.
- Expect that they may seek solace through isolation rather than social contact.
- Expect a general increased sensitivity. For example, they may be quicker to anger than usual or sensory sensitivities may be amplified.
- Expect a rise in pre-existing self-stimulatory behaviors (for example, rocking, tapping, flicking) or special interests, both of which can have a calming influence.
- Don't be afraid if they show an intense interest in the subject of death and if they seek 'the facts' surrounding a death. (Autism Alliance with Permission from Autism Spectrum Australia's "Aspect," 2023)

ALEX AND MY MOM, HIS GRANDMA, DOROTHY HAM, AT ALEX'S FORSYTH CENTRAL HIGH SCHOOL BACCALAUREATE SERVICE 2016

I truly believe psychologists can help, as can art therapists, therapeutic recreation, music therapy, and the like. I have a friend whose adult daughter with autism makes the most fabulous of art pieces, and has experienced her own trauma in life, the whole family did, in other ways, and the work this woman with autism displays at galleries provides more vivid communication of her thoughts and feelings than any professional orator could ever share. But, yeah, what scares me so much in this world, is for Alex to be without one of us . . .his mom and dad or both . . . and I'm thinking we aren't alone in our fears.

Resources

- **"Grief and Bereavement Resources for People with Autism" from Autism Speaks https://www.autismspeaks.org/grief-and-bereavement-resources**

References

Grief and loss resources (2023). Autism Alliance. https://www.autismalliance.org/grief-and-loss-resources

Chapter 16 - Caregivers and Wellness

Just this year I was discharged from my cardiologist's office following my yearly follow-up: I left with a big grin from him and the staff as the results of my stress test and echo show that I "have the heart of an athlete." It wasn't always this way. As parents and caregivers of children on the autism spectrum (and all special needs) know, the stress of raising a child with autism, a child with a disability, takes great toll on our physical, mental, social, financial well-being. Some people can't eat when they are stressed, and some of us go full Hostess Cupcakes Monty. I have always loved food—it signifies to me family, community, friends, tradition. It also is my go-to when I am stressed—a Snickers, a doughnut, a Captain D's fried everything sampler (A Southeastern United States fast seafood restaurant). I also know and appreciate the cost of a McDs and Wendy's value menu meal item or a $5 Little Caesar's Hot and Ready.

As Alex's mom, the stress from doctor's appointments, schools, meltdowns, and cost—yes, we chose to go full intense early intervention with Alex's diagnosis in 2000, but it also, by 2007, in the wake of drowning medical bills and all things recession Michigan, caused us to declare bankruptcy and foreclose on our home. Navigating resources: social security, assists of food from our county community health department, trying to find a place to live, while still being positively engaged with our son in all facets of his life, plus the stigma you feel as you watch your friends and family's kids soar, participate in sports, art, music, dance, heck, even get potty trained before age 6 and 12 (we did it in stages), watching normal developmental milestones be met that you know your child may never not (I was my son's chauffer to college!), let alone everything else involved as a role not only as parent, but as at home medical, educational caregiver while trying to manage your own jobs, relationships will wreak havoc on your body.

I have liver disease (early scarring cirrhosis), Hashimoto, alopecia areata, lung disease (constrictive bronchiolitis, cysts, mosaic lung disease), migraines, skin flare ups, Raynaud's Syndrome, fatigue, anxiety, and multiple orthopedic surgeries, all common with those who live with intense mental and physical stress from being a caregiver to a special needs child, so I have come to a point in my life, and where I hope you can all reach as well, to focus on wellbeing. Yes, I recognize we all deserve a trip monthly to a spa, an exotic vacation, but for the majority of us, that isn't happening. I go to 24 Hour Fitness near me in downtown Portland Oregon (they have a hot tub!), and I know that at Planet Fitness—you can go for as little as $10 a month, but I also go for a walk—it's free! And do breathing and meditation exercises—many of which you can find for free in iTunes and Google Play. I do yoga via Netflix and Amazon Prime (they have many free great "restorative" yoga options)—and with the yoga—I can do it at home, no need for childcare. I also love water, and anywhere we live I search for activities I can do near water: read or go for a walk. In Portland I am on a Dragon Boat team for $130 a year. Find what you love. I love a cheap cup of coffee and a book or word game.

I now also try to mostly focus on eating "whole foods"—an egg is one, a doughnut is not (but I honestly treat myself to those, too—my local bakery even has vegan ones). In the era before Covid, my husband worked weekly out of state, which left me the at home parent; I drank a lot of pre-made protein drinks: Walmart and Costco have great affordable store brands ones (and honestly I still do); I eat protein bars—these

options are fast, easy, on the go. I pre-make meals. I have a great veggie chili slow cooker, instant pot recipe; I will pre-make Alex's favorite baked salmon (you can get affordable cheap frozen salmon at Walmart). And yes, I still do a Hot and Ready Pizza via Little Caesar; honestly, almost every Friday night—an easy go to choice, but I also know that Walmart has very affordable produce, and I'm all about store brands, our local Safeway does as well. Most importantly, you must treat yourself. Personally, I'm not much of a TV watcher, but I love music, and I can happily spend an eve walking the neighborhood listening to my free Pandora Madonna channel, or dancing in my kitchen to Motown. In later years, when our kids with autism became adults, my friends and I—six of us—all moms of young adult sons with autism from Louisiana to California to Oregon, have created a traveling sisters

THE LUGGAGE GANG 2022 (FRONT ROW LEFT TO RIGHT: ELEANOR, DAWN HAM-KUCHARSKI. BACK ROW: MARIANNE, SUZI, CAROLYN, AND MEGAN)

group: The Luggage Gang. We speak almost every day since our boys were little: phones, email, yahoo groups, Facebook ones, Messenger, and once a year we meet up somewhere in the United States for a vacation: an Airbnb and adventures. I can't begin to even say how much they motivate me, inspire me, lift me up, rescue me, and refresh me. Find your peeps. Open up to others. You aren't alone. I promise. Remember, to be the best person you can be for your loved one with autism, that you also must love yourself and listen to your body . . . stress talks loudly—in many physical forms. Do not ignore that—I did for years, and I was oh so wrong . . .

Chapter 17 - Marriage and Relationships

For autism awareness month in April, we shine blue. Blue lights on porches show our support, and we should also shine that same light on honesty of the strain autism can have on the family. There are so many truths to what a family and individual with autism faces, and one of them deals with the high divorce rate. As a family, we have done a few rounds of family counseling, but Rich and I, besides facilitating separate support groups for mothers, wives and dads and husbands of those affected by autism, we have also, together, and separately, had rounds of marriage counseling and have been separated twice...in 2005 and 2012, even going as far as filing for divorce, but eventually canceling that procedure.

I love my husband, and he loves me. Rich is my best friend, but as a parent or caregiver of a special need's child, you often forget the importance of focusing on the spouse, your partner, on yourself, as the strain of caregiving depletes the both of you. You make wrong choices under great stress. I have. Rich has. You can also say hurtful things. I remember one time when Alex was four, I honestly, in a moment of meltdown, told Rich "when I look at you, all I see is a health insurance card." And that was hurtful to him. Our love and friendship, which we've had since we were teens, and our always returning to each other...plus some phenomenal therapists...such as Rabbi Ben of Piscataway NJ, has kept us strong.

Remember that you deserve to focus on your relationship as well as your child. Respite providers, therapists, honesty, all this you have earned, and for those who

RICH AND I: PROM 1990

ultimately found the crack of the stress of ASD on their marriage too hard to repair, Rich and I have walked along almost similar fault lines and remember to focus on you. Therapy helped Rich and I not just as a couple, but as individuals. We were equal in the almost dissolution of our marriage and family, and honestly, I look back on all this with no regret. Those journeys made us, myself: stronger, and we have taught Alex much by our shining a blue light of honesty with him about the mountains we climb in life.

RICH AND I DECEMBER 2022

Chapter 18 – Friends

Every day, parents and caregivers of autism need a break. A nap. A glass of wine (A Manhattan if you are Rich; Margarita if you are me). Sometimes more than a glass. A friend to listen, understand, and often that same friend is stuck being parental "caregiver" and hearing the same fears, concerns, stories, over and over, from us, and we appreciate you, so so so so much. Because of you, we can be the best we can be for our child on the spectrum. You take the time; you care; you have our back. When we fall, you pick us up. When we need to get away, you whisk us to an adventure. And we have family who do this, too—I'm tossing you under the friends umbrella because you are our lifelong forever friends—and also family—double perk for us.

WITH OUR HAM FAMILY: L-R FRONT ROW: ME, ALEX'S COUSINS: EMMALINE, CAROLINE, ALEX'S AUNT JACKIE; BACK ROW: ALEX, RICH (MY HUSBAND AND ALEX'S DAD), ALEX'S UNCLE DAVE

Dawn Ham-Kucharski

WITH OUR KUCHARSKI FAMILY: STARTING AT HEAD OF TABLE AND GOING TO LEFT SIDE AND DOWN RIGHT: RICH, ALEX'S COUSIN PRESTON, ALEX'S AUNT ANN, MYSELF, ALEX, ALEX'S COUSIN EVAN, ALEX'S COUSIN DAKOTA

And to new parents and caregivers of those with autism, please, I know it is hard, you at first fill with guilt at "me" time but take that break. Before covid, when my husband, Rich, traveled during the week. . . my rule was: "Alex, I love you but after 9 p.m. it is my time" (during the week). Now, I get that is way easier with a then 21-year-old with autism than a 2, 4, 15-year-old with ASD—been there my friends, and I send you a bouquet of chocolate—the really fun kind you would feel guilty about enjoying—say a package of Oreos—it is on me. I was also up by 5 am—again—my time, and easier because I had a high functioning adult on the spectrum (but it wasn't always that way), and in the past, I was a perfectionist, a control freak, but the early morns, before work, before school, before autism can jump out of its comfort zone Jack-in-the-Box—the before sunrise time was mine and still is: sometimes it is reading, sometimes playing a word game, catching up on social media, and it usually always involves exercise: a walk, yoga in front of my fire place with Amazon Prime, some meditation, a trip to the gym. Sometimes just herbal tea, a great bowl of oatmeal, and snuggled with blankets. That is mine. That is my time.

 Find that time and go out with your friends; they will listen—help you to let go, and provide you with well-deserved mental health break and wellness in all the forms that can take. And I'll be honest, sometimes I'm so caught up in the "Alexisms" and the "Dawnisms" I forget to ask my friend, "Hey, how are you?" "What are your kids, work, husband, partner, pet up to?" And guess what, they need you, too, and when your friend shows that they need you, that they need your input, your advice, you show they matter, and that you do, too. So, a huge thank you to our friends, from all states we have lived, all the places we have been, those who remind me that "Life is Good" (To quote a girlfriend of mine in Georgia—who the rest of the world borrowed this quote from). . . I love you; I appreciate you, and because you have taught me to focus on happiness and well-being, that I matter . . . I snuggle each night in bed with a book and a cup of tea . . . and take an autism break . . .

Chapter 19 – Conclusion

Rich and I wish to thank the friends and family who have been there for all three of Team HK and especially for Alex. To be honest, there were some family and friends we walked away from, who couldn't love our son for who he is, for which autism is a huge part, but way more than those few have stood by our sides, since the day my mom, my sister-in-law Jackie, Alex, and I sat at the University of Michigan, in a small clinic, in September of 2000, and Dr. Rick Solomon told us that Alex had moderate to severe autism, but if we trusted him, Alex would, by 3rd grade, be living successfully with ASD...and that story became truth. You've heard our stories, our thoughts, our plans, our ups, our downs, our truths, but that blue light on our porch shines (literally and figuratively) for all with autism and their families, friends, and the teachers, therapists, doctors who hold all of those affected by ASD's hands, give hope, learn new perspectives, and give so much love, and with that, as I conclude, I'd love to hear your stories, experiences, emotions, and be there for you and your children, your work and life experiences, just as you have done for us. You can share them to my email at DawnhkSpectrumJourney@gmail.com . Those blue lights framing our front door, are shining for you to come in...

Some Concluding Resources

- **Applying for Social Security Disability for Children Under 18 with Autism and Adults with Autism**
  https://paautism.org/resource/social-security/
- **Grandin, T., & Moore, D. (2022).** *The Loving Push, 2nd Edition: A Guide to Successfully Prepare Spectrum Kids for Adulthood (2nd ed.).***: Future Horizons.** https://www.amazon.com/Loving-Push-Temple-Grandin/dp/1949177742/ref=sr_1_14?crid=6UK4NEUY1KXI&keywords=temple+grandin&qid=1676836975&sprefix=temple+%2Caps%2C502&sr=8-14
- **Job Training Skills via Easter Seals**
  https://www.easterseals.com/programs-and-services/adult-services/

- **Reminder from an above section that an individual with autism can soar, if we all live by these words of Holocaust survivor Viktor Frankl:**
  https://www.youtube.com/watch?v=UgVA6nXCj1U

Epilogue

All thanks goes to Alex, for allowing his mom to share his story, and stepping away from his (and our) story, I can't help but reflect on all of the things we were told Alex would never do: Alex would never talk, and he does—despite stumbles in expressive speech, his receptive speech and written voice are both strong—and he enjoys discussing politics, culture, religion, science and video gaming. Alex as a young child was expected to remain in a self-contained classroom through age 26 in Michigan and receive a certificate; instead, he has graduated from high school with a diploma; and graduated with a Bachelors of Arts Degree from Portland State University with a major in International and Global Studies with an Asian Concentration and Japanese Language in December of 2022 with a 3.6 GPA; We were told that Alex would never be social—he is!; Alex would lack empathy for others—he is one of the kindest caring individuals I know whether in regard to humans, animals, and our planet (Alex has been volunteering with us for a variety of non-profits since he was three years old—As an elementary student, he was my co-chair for Relay for Life—take your loved ones with Autism with you—out in the community—to serve or observe—even for a few minutes—you and they will be so proud!). We were also told that Alex would never live independently—yet he has—two weeks in Atlanta attending SCAD summer workshops when he was 16; Memorial Day weekend 2018—for three days, solo, navigating Atlanta hotels, restaurants and Momocon; and at age 20—five weeks in Japan in Osaka, Hiroshima, and Tokyo. And while I understand that all our children with autism have different paths and destinies, I know that I am a better person, teacher, wife, family member, friend, because of the nuances of perspective having a child with autism has given me. Rich and I are blessed with a best friend, a son, who may or may not always live with us, who adores all animals, is a video game guru, loves to learn, and is active in his community . . . and he happens to have autism.

About the Author

Dawn Ham-Kucharski , a proud Eastern Michigan University alumnus with Bachelors and Master's degrees in studies of literature, history, and religious studies, and a former English professor, lives with her husband, Rich; her son, Alex; and the most amazing neighbors in downtown Portland Oregon, where she enjoys writing; the world's best coffee and doughnuts; taking an immense number of photos; laughing with her friends; paddling with her dragon boat and outrigger canoe teammates on the Willamette River; and exploring the Northwest Coast with her family. She is the co-author, along with S. Jhoanna Robledo, of *The Autism Book: Answers to Your Most Pressing Questions*.

Contributors

Alex Ham-Kucharski is a recent graduate of Portland State University with a Bachelor of Arts Degree in International and Global Studies: Asian Studies with Japanese Language. A published researcher on PDX Scholar, he also has performed in kabuki as a dancer and percussionist. Alex is also a Graduate Student in the Masters in Nonprofit Leadership program at Portland State University. In addition, he enjoys video gaming, *Nat Geo Wild*, travel, being the pizza connoisseur of Portland OR, and exploring zoos, aquariums, and museums, and is a *Jurassic Park*, *Star Wars*, and *Harry Potter* aficionado.

Rich Ham-Kucharski has a Bachelor of Science in Economics from Eastern Michigan University. While not designing Cloud and Application Systems for Slalom Consulting, he volunteers with the Portland Police Bureau Advisory Council and We Shine and competes at the state and national level in Powerlifting. A former Special Olympics coach in bowling, shot put, and powerlifting, Rich enjoys travel and science fiction films and watching anything *Star Wars* with his family.

www.ingramcontent.com/pod-product-compliance
Lightning Source LLC
Chambersburg PA
CBHW050648250726
48662CB00002B/561